SENTENCE CONSTRUCTION
Writing and Combining Standard English Sentences

Book I

Alice C. Pack   Lynn E. Henrichsen

Brigham Young University
Hawaii Campus

Newbury House Publishers, Inc. / Rowley / Massachusetts / 01969
1980

Library of Congress Cataloging in Publication Data

Pack, Alice C
   Writing and combining standard English sentences.

   SUMMARY: Text and exercises outline how to write grammatically-correct expository sentences.
   CONTENTS: [1] Sentence construction.
   1. English language--Text-books for foreigners.
2. English language--Composition and exercises.
3. English language--Sentences. [1. English language--Sentences. 2. English language--Composition and exercises] I. Henrichsen, Lynn E., joint author. II. Title.
PE1128.P23   428.2'4   80-19507
ISBN 0-88377-173-X (v. 1)

Cover and book design by DIANA ESTERLY.

NEWBURY HOUSE PUBLISHERS, INC.

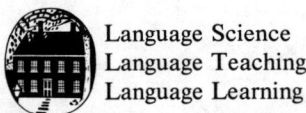
Language Science
Language Teaching
Language Learning

ROWLEY, MASSACHUSETTS 01969

Copyright © 1980 by Newbury House Publishers, Inc. All rights reserved. No part of this book may be reproduced or transmitted in any form or by any means, electronic or mechanical, including photocopying, recording, or by any information storage and retrieval system, without permission in writing from the Publisher.

First printing: August 1980

Printed in the U.S.A.   5   4

TABLE OF CONTENTS

		To the Teacher	v
Chapter 1.		**WORD TYPES AND FORMS**	
	1.	Content and Function Words	1
	2.	Content Words and Derivational Classes	2
	3.	Content Words and Inflectional Forms	4
Chapter 2.		**NOUNS**	
	1.	Types of Nouns	9
	2.	Nouns and Unit Expressions	12
	3.	Articles and Nouns (Nonspecific)	13
	4.	Articles and Nouns (Specific)	15
	5.	Expressions of Quantity with *a*	17
	6.	Articles and Proper Nouns	18
Chapter 3.		**PRONOUNS**	
	1.	Purpose of Pronouns	22
	2.	Pronoun Agreement with Antecedents	23
	3.	Clarity of Pronoun Antecedents	26
	4.	Dummy Subjects	28
Chapter 4.		**AUX-WORDS**	
	1.	Forms of Aux-words	32
	2.	Subject/Aux-word Agreement (Present Tense)	33
	3.	Subject/Aux-word Agreement (Past Tense)	38
	4.	Yes/No Questions and Aux-words	39
	5.	Hidden Aux-words	43
	6.	Negatives and Aux-words	50
	7.	Verb/Aux-word Look-Alikes	51
	8.	Aux-word Modals	52
Chapter 5.		**VERB FORMS AND THEIR USES**	
	1.	English Verb Forms	57
	2.	Present Time-included Forms and Their Uses	61
	3.	Past Time-included Forms and Their Uses	64
	4.	Timeless Verb Forms and Their Uses	66
	5.	Multiple Aux-word/Verb Combinations	70

	6. Two-word Verbs	72
	7. Separable and Inseparable Two-word Verbs	74

Chapter 6. **VERBS AND TIME**

1.	Establishing Time	79
2.	The Simple Present Tense and Time	80
3.	The Simple Past Tense and Time	81
4.	The *-ing* Verb Form and Time	83
5.	The Earlier-than-established-time Relationship	87
6.	The Later-than-established-time Relationship	90
7.	Summary of Time and Tense Relationships	93
8.	Later or Earlier Time with *-ing* Forms	95
9.	Modal + Have Combinations	98

Chapter 7. **THE SENTENCE**

1.	Subject and Predicate	102
2.	Simple and Complex Sentences	104
3.	Shifters	105
4.	Basic Sentence Patterns	108
5.	Sentence Pattern Number One	111
6.	Sentence Pattern Number Two	112
7.	Transitive/Intransitive Verbs	113
8.	Sentence Pattern Number Three	115
9.	Sentence Pattern Number Four	117
10.	Summary of Sentence Patterns	118
11.	*Wh-*Questions	119

Chapter 8. **MODIFIERS**

1.	The Nucleus of the Noun Phrase	123
2.	Order of Noun Modifiers	123
3.	Singular and Plural Forms of Modifiers	126
4.	The Modifier *Very*	126
5.	Adjective Complement Modifiers	126
6.	Verb Forms Used as Modifiers	129
7.	Comparative Forms of Adjectives	132
8.	Superlative Forms of Adjectives	136
9.	Nouns Used as Modifiers	139
10.	Phrases and Clauses Used as Modifiers	139
11.	Adverbs of Frequency and Probability	141
12.	Adverbs of Intensity	142
13.	Adverbs of Manner, Place, Time, etc.	144

Appendix A.	**CONTENT WORDS**	149
Appendix B.	**SOME COMMON NONCOUNT NOUNS AND UNIT EXPRESSIONS**	153
Appendix C.	**IRREGULAR VERB FORMS**	154
Appendix D.	**SOME COMMON TWO-WORD VERBS**	156

TO THE TEACHER

This book is not an all-inclusive treatment of English grammar. (For such, teachers and students are referred to any of the several reference grammars or handbooks of English available on the market.) Rather, it is a review text which covers the persistent errors that intermediate and advanced students of English as a second language (ESL) and standard English as a second dialect (SESD) make when writing.

The primary purpose of this volume and its companion, *Sentence Combination,* is to teach students to write grammatically correct, expository prose of the type generally expected in academic situations. The focus is on the sentence, although contextually connected exercises are used throughout the book.

In *Sentence Construction,* student production is limited to writing basic sentences. The companion volume to this book, *Sentence Combination,* teaches numerous transforming and combining techniques which students can employ to produce complexity and variety in their writing.

Some grammatical explanations are based on Robert L. Allen's sector-analysis. Others, dealing with verbs and time, are based on the English tense-aspect system. Whenever useful, traditional grammatical terms or sector-analysis terms have been employed. In other cases, these terms have been modified, or new, more descriptive terms have been coined. In all cases, student receptivity has been kept in mind and the most descriptive term has been used.

Throughout the book, brief explanations, accompanied by explanatory charts and diagrams, are followed by sets of assignments. These explanations are limited to what is pedagogically feasible in the normal classroom. Examples, which help students understand each rule, are given, but most learning will take place as students work through the assignments. The wealth of examples and practice precludes the need for excessively detailed explanation.

All assignments consist of contextualized passages. (For convenience in referring to particular sentences, the individual sentences in each passage have been numbered consecutively.) Assignments usually follow a pattern of (1) recognition of the grammatical concept/construction, (2) limited/guided production in specific areas, and (3) original writing.

Sentence Construction can be used in a variety of ways.

1. The traditional **chapter-by-chapter approach** may be followed. This approach assures coverage of the basic grammatical foundations of standard written English.
2. Each chapter can also be treated as an **individual module**. In this approach, students—individually or as a class—are referred to particular chapters after diagnosis of their individual problems. Diagnostic materials for this purpose are provided in this text and its companion volume, *Sentence Combination.*
3. Although the order of presentation used in the book—explanation, followed by examples, followed by practice—suggests a **deductive approach** to learning, this order can be modified by teachers who prefer to teach in an **inductive manner,** presenting examples first and then encouraging students to formulate rules before referring to the textual explanations.
4. A **spiral approach** is also practicable due to the fact that all exercises are presented in sets of three (A, B, and C). The A exercises may be assigned in the first cycle, the B's used in the next, and the C's reserved for later use or review.

Instruction should emphasize a high standard of correctness in writing. When exercises focus on a particular grammatical point and require completion only, mastery must be demanded if students are to produce correct, original writing in later sections.

Students who have persistent problems with prepositions, pronouns, determiners, or verb forms and choices should be assigned individual, out-of-class work in the appropriate area of the *Dyad Learning Program.*

A NOTE ON SENTENCE COMBINING

Considerable research regarding the value of sentence combining in the classroom has been reported in recent years. Numerous studies have suggested that sentence-combining activities stimulate the development of syntactic maturity. Many successful teachers of writing have used sentence combining in various types of exercises with results as varied as the methods and techniques used.

Teachers who desire to learn more about experimental research involving sentence-combining, including its history, rationale, and current findings, are referred to the following bibliography.

Christensen, Frances. 1968. The problem of defining a mature style. *English Journal* 57: 572–579.
Combs, Warren E. 1976. Further effects of sentence-combining practice on writing ability. *Research in the Teaching of English* 10: 137–149.
Crymes, Ruth. 1971. The relation of study about language to language performance: with special reference to nominalization. *TESOL Quarterly* 5, 3: 217–230.
Daiker, Donald, Kerek, Andrew, and Morenberg, Max. 1978. Sentence-combining and syntactic maturity. *College Composition and Communication* 29, 1: 36–41.
Daiker, Donald, Kerek, Andrew, and Morenberg, Max, eds. 1979. *Sentence combining and the teaching of writing.* Akron: L & S Books.
Endicott, Anthony L. 1973. A proposed scale for syntactic complexity. *Research in the Teaching of English* 7: 5–12.
Faigley, Lester L. 1979. Generative rhetoric as a way of increasing syntactic fluency. *College Composition and Communication* 30: 176–181.
Hunt, Kellogg W. 1966. Recent measures in syntactic development. *Elementary English* 43: 732–739. (Also in Mark Lester, ed. 1973. *Readings in applied transformational grammar,* 2nd ed. New York: Holt, Rinehart and Winston.)
Hunt, Kellogg W. 1967. How little sentences grow into big ones. In *New directions in elementary English,* ed. Alexander Frazier. Champaign: National Council of Teachers of English. (Also in Mark Lester, ed. See Hunt, 1966 above.)
Hunt, Kellogg W. 1970. Do sentences in the second language grow like those in the first? *TESOL Quarterly* 4, 3: 195–202.
Hunt, Kellogg W. 1970. *Syntactic maturity in schoolchildren and adults. Monographs of the society for research in child development,* No. 134. Chicago: University of Chicago Press.
Hunt, Kellogg W. 1977. Early blooming and late blooming syntactic structures. In *Evaluating writing: describing, measuring, judging.* Champaign: National Council of Teachers of English.
Mellon, John. 1967. Transformational sentence combining: a method for enhancing the development of syntactic fluency in English composition. Final Report, Cooperative Research Project No. 5-8418. Office of English Education and Laboratory for Research in Instruction. Graduate School of Education, Harvard University, Cambridge, Massachusetts. (See also: Same title as above. NCTE research report #10. Champaign: National Council of Teachers of English.)
Morenberg, Max, Daiker, Donald, and Kerek, Andrew. 1978. Sentence combining at the college level: an experimental study. *Research in the Teaching of English* 12: 245–256.
O'Donnell, Roy C., Griffin, William J., and Norris, Raymond C. 1967. Syntax of kindergarten and elementary school children: a transformational analysis. NCTE research report #8. Champaign: National Council of Teachers of English.
O'Hare, Frank. 1973. Sentence combining: improving student writing without formal grammar. NCTE reserach report #15. Champaign: National Council of Teachers of English.
Shook, Ron. 1978. Sentence combining: a theory and two reviews. *TESL Reporter* 11, 3: 4–7, 12, and 15.
Stevick, Earl. 1966. *A workbook in language teaching: with special reference to English as a foreign language.* New York: Abingdon Press, pp. 60–66.
Stotsky, Sandra L. 1975. Sentence-combining as a curricular activity: its effect on written language development and reading comprehension. *Research in the Teaching of English* 9: 30–71.
Strong, William. 1976. Sentence-combining: back to the basics and beyond. *English Journal* 65: 60–64.
Swan, M. Beverly. 1979. Sentence combining in college composition: interim measures and patterns. *Research in the Teaching of English* 13, 3: 217–224.
Weiser, Irwin. 1979. Sentence combining for diction and detail improvement. *Freshman English Resource Notes* 4, 3: 8–9 and 12.

STUDENT DIAGNOSIS AND REFERRAL

The following diagnostic materials may be useful to teachers who wish to use the individualized approach mentioned in the "To the Teacher" section of this book. As the first step in the student diagnosis and referral procedure, students write a short essay on a topic which calls for the use of different times, various forms of modifiers, comparison, transition, etc. Three example topics follow:

Write about your education. Where have you gone to school before? What are you studying now? When do you expect to finish? What are you going to do after that? How will you be different because of your educational experience?

Briefly describe your daily life when you were a young child and your daily life now. Then, explain the more important similarities and differences between them.

Write a description of something unusual that you have done recently or something unusual that has happened to you. Compare it with what you expected to do or expected to happen. Then tell what you expect to do in the future as a result of this unusual experience.

After students have written their essays, the instructor/tutor analyzes the errors and checks the appropriate categories on the diagnostic/referral checklist provided at the end of this section. The subheadings in each category may be circled to indicate specific problems.

The bracketed numbers following each category on the checklist refer to chapters in *Sentence Construction* and *Sentence Combination* which treat the particular problems listed in the category. (The *Dyad Learning Program* materials are separate Newbury House publications.) After diagnosis, students should be assigned work in the chapters/sections indicated on the checklist.

Other diagnostic methods and materials may also be used. A progressive diagnosis may be conducted by using one of the three assignments which follow each grammar explanation as a diagnostic exercise for the grammar point covered in that section. Other diagnostic materials, such as cloze passages keyed to specific errors (to facilitate referral) and/or sentence completion exercises, which call for the use of a variety of grammatical constructions and times, may also be used. Examples of each follow:

Cloze Passage

For centuries men have wondered how man acquired or developed languages. Scholars still speculate on where [and] how man got his words. [One] linguist asserts that this has [occasioned] more interest and speculation, probably, [than] any other single aspect of [the] whole language problem. During the [eighteenth] and nineteenth centuries so much [attention] was addressed to this subject [that] the French Academy of Science [passed] a rule formally excluding any [more] communications on this topic from [its] transactions.

Theories of language origin [have] included the onomatopoetic or "bow-wow" [theory], or the idea that language [began] with imitations of sounds occurring [in] nature; the "ding-dong" theory which [maintains] there is a mystic correlation [between] sound and meaning; the "pooh-pooh" [theory] which holds that speech first [consisted] of reactions to fear, pleasure, [pain], etc.; the "yo-he-ho" theory which [asserts] that grunts from physical exertion [originated] language; and the "ta-ta" theory [which] poses that vocal organs unconsciously [attempted] to mimic bodily actions or [mimic] gestures of the hands.

viii SENTENCE CONSTRUCTION

    As __[more]__ and more languages are analyzed, __[and]__ extensive information on language becomes __[available]__, the faultier all these theories __[that]__ language evolved from imitative sounds __[or]__ primitive grunts and groans seem. Primitive languages are, as a rule, anything but primitive except with reference to modern civilization's vocabulary.

Exact words answers are given in brackets. Other contextually and grammatically appropriate responses should also be accepted. Incorrect responses should be analyzed and reported on the diagnostic/referal checklist.

Sentence Completion Exercise

Complete the sentences below. Make certain that your sentences are contextually connected in a meaningful way. In other words, write a story.

1. Some of my friends usually

2. While they do that, I sometimes

3. Although my mother

4. However, my father always

5. Our neighbors have never

6. Every day they

7. Their children

8. Even their dog and cat

9. In the past, we

10. Now we only

11. In the future

As with the essay and cloze passage, student errors made in the sentence completion exercise should be analyzed using the categories on the diagnostic/referral checklist.

Diagnostic/Referral Checklist

    WORD DERIVATIONS (Forms of Content Words) [1]
        Noun, verb, adjective, and adverb form confusion/misuse

    ARTICLES [2 and *Dyad Learning Program: Determiners*]
        Incorrect choice; unnecessarily used; omitted when needed

    NOUNS [2]
        Singular-plural or count-noncount confusion/misuse; failure to use proper unit expression with noncount noun

    PRONOUNS [3 and *Dyad Learning Program: Pronouns*]
        Lack of agreement with antecedent; ambiguous antecedent; no antecedent; unnecessarily used; not used when called for; incorrect form

    AUXILIARIES AND MODALS (Aux-words) [4]
        Incorrect choice; omitted when needed; unnecessarily used

    VERB FORMS [5, 7, and *Dyad Learning Program: Verb Forms and Verb Choices*]
        Incorrect form (base, *d-t-n*, *-ing* +*s*, no-*s*, past); incorrect verb choice; unnecessarily used; omitted when needed; incorrect use of two-word verbs

    VERB/AUX-AGREEMENT WITH SUBJECT (Harmony, Concord) [4, 5, 8:1 and *Dyad Learning Program: Verb Forms*]
        +*s*/no-*s* confusion; ignorance of true nucleus of noun phrase

    VERB/AUX-AGREEMENT WITH TIME [6 and 13:6]
        Lack of agreement with general context, with time signal, with other verbs, in complete sentences, and/or with compound noun clauses

    MODIFIERS [8]
        Incorrect form (*-ing/d-t-n*, adjective/adverb, etc.); incorrect order; incorrect position in sentence

    COMPARATIVES AND SUPERLATIVES [8:7, 8:8]
        Inappropriate comparison; incorrect comparative formation, inappropriate superlative; incorrect superlative formation

    BASIC SENTENCE STRUCTURE [7]
        Incorrect syntax (word order); incorrect shifter; omitted object with transitive verb

    EXPLETIVES *there* or *it* (Dummy Subjects) [3:4, 13]
        Unnecessarily used; omitted when needed; followed by incorrect form of verb/aux-word

    INCOMPLETE SENTENCES (Fragments) [7, 8, 11, and 12]
        Omission of subject; omission of verb; prepositional phrase used alone; subordinate clause used alone; noun phrase used alone; half-sentence used alone

    COORDINATION (Compounding) [10]
        Run-on sentences; comma splice; faulty parallelism, incorrect conjunction choice; incorrect compounding method; unnecessary repetition

    SUBORDINATE CLAUSES [11]
        Incorrect clause formation; poor relationship to main sentence; incorrect subordinator

    RELATIVE CLAUSES [11]
        Incorrect clause formation; poor relationship to modified noun; incorrect relative pronoun

    HALF-SENTENCES (Participial Phrases, Absolute Phrases) [12]
        Incorrect formation; poor relationship to main sentence; different subjects

    NOMINAL CLAUSES OR PHRASES [13]
        Incorrect clause formation; incorrect introducer or substitutor; poor relationship; *-ing/to* + base form misuse/confusion

    PASSIVE TRANSFORMATION [9:1]
        Used inappropriately; incorrect formation

    INDIRECT OBJECT TRANSFORMATION [9:2]
        Used inappropriately; incorrect formation

    TRANSITION WORDS [15:1]
        Not used when called for; used inappropriately; poor or incorrect choice

    VARIETY IN WRITING [7, 12:7, and 15:2]
        Insufficient variety of basic sentence patterns; insufficient variety of combining methods

    COMMAS [7:3, 10, 11, 12, 14]
        Incorrect use with shifters; comma splice; incorrect use with relative clauses; incorrect use with half-sentences; incorrect use with (non-restrictive) added information

    VOCABULARY [All Chapters]
        Too limited; incorrect word choice

    PREPOSITIONS [*Dyad Learning Program: Prepositions*]
        Incorrect choice; omitted when needed; unnecessarily used

    OTHER PROBLEMS

x SENTENCE CONSTRUCTION

ESSAY #1

English Second Language

Briefly explain how you studied English before you came here. Then, explain how you plan to study English now. Finally, point out some of the differences and similarities between your two methods of studying English.

One of the greatest links that helps to <u>unit</u> [spelling] all the <u>variety</u> [word derivation] tribes in my country <u>are</u> [verb/aux agreement w/subj.; ignorance of true nucleus] the common usage of ₍△₎ [article omitted] English language. I began the study of ₍△₎ [article omitted] English language during my fourth year in primary school. <u>Among</u> [preposition incorrect] other pupils, I began to learn some English names for both proper and common nouns.

In 1969, I passed the entrance to <u>Grammar School</u> [capitalization]. I spent five years in <u>the</u> [article unnecessary] grammar school ₍△₎ [comma omitted non-restrictive] <u>which</u> [subordinator incorrect] English is the medium of <u>instructions</u> [noun count/noncount]. In <u>the</u> [article unnecessary] grammar school, my learning of English advanced much <u>more than the primary school</u> [comparison inappropriate]. <u>It was in</u> [expletive unnecessary] grammar <u>School</u> [capitalization], I learnt to do comprehension and precis. My study of ₍△₎ [article omitted] Latin language for five years helped me <u>a great</u> [modifier] <u>deal</u> [position] to improve my <u>vocabularies</u> [noun count/noncount]. I arrived <u>at</u> [preposition unnecessary] here to meet ₍△₎ [article omitted] <u>entialy</u> [spelling] different method of learning English. It is my candid opinion that the visual <u>aid</u> [noun s/p] and method of teaching English here <u>is</u> [verb/aux agreement with subject] of immense assistance to <u>we</u> [pronoun incorrect form] foreign students.

Diagnostic/Referral Checklist

_____ ✓_____ **WORD DERIVATIONS** (Forms of Content Words) [1]
   Noun, verb, adjective, and adverb form confusion/misuse

_✓✓✓✓✓_____ **ARTICLES** [2 and *Dyad Learning Program: Determiners*]
   Incorrect choice; <u>unnecessarily used</u>; <u>omitted when needed</u>

_____ ✓✓✓ _____ **NOUNS** [2]
   <u>Singular-plural</u> or <u>count-noncount confusion/misuse</u>; failure to use proper unit expression with noncount noun

_____ ✓ _____ **PRONOUNS** [3 and *Dyad Learning Program: Pronouns*]
   Lack of agreement with antecedent; ambiguous antecedent; no antecedent; unnecessarily used; not used when called for; <u>incorrect form</u>

_____ **AUXILIARIES AND MODALS** (Aux-words) [4]
   Incorrect choice; omitted when needed; unnecessarily used

_____ **VERB FORMS** [5, 7, and *Dyad Learning Program: Verb Forms and Verb Choices*]
   Incorrect form (base, <u>d-t-n</u>, <u>-ing</u> +<u>s</u>, no-<u>s</u>, past); incorrect verb choice; unnecessarily used; omitted when needed; incorrect use of two-word verbs

_____ ✓✓ _____ **VERB/AUX-AGREEMENT WITH SUBJECT** (Harmony, Concord) [4, 5, 8:1 and *Dyad Learning Program: Verb Forms*]
   +s/no-s confusion; <u>ignorance of true nucleus of noun phrase</u>

_____ **VERB/AUX-AGREEMENT WITH TIME** [6 and 13:6]
   Lack of agreement with general context, with time signal, with other verbs, in complete sentences, and/or with compound noun clauses

_____ ✓ _____ **MODIFIERS** [8]
   Incorrect form (-*ing*/*d-t-n*, adjective/adverb, etc.); incorrect order; <u>incorrect position in sentence</u>

_____ ✓ _____ **COMPARATIVES AND SUPERLATIVES** [8:7, 8:8]
   <u>Inappropriate comparison</u>; incorrect comparative formation, inappropriate superlative; incorrect superlative formation

_____ **BASIC SENTENCE STRUCTURE** [7]
   Incorrect syntax (word order); incorrect shifter; omitted object with transitive verb

_____ ✓ _____ **EXPLETIVES** *there* or *it* (Dummy Subjects) [3:4, 13]
   <u>Unnecessarily used</u>; omitted when needed; followed by incorrect form of verb/aux-word

_____ **INCOMPLETE SENTENCES** (Fragments) [7, 8, 11, and 12]
   Omission of subject; omission of verb; prepositional phrase used alone; subordinate clause used alone; noun phrase used alone; half-sentence used alone

_____ **COORDINATION** (Compounding) [10]
   Run-on sentences; comma splice; faulty parallelism, incorrect conjunction choice; incorrect compounding method; unnecessary repetition

_____ ✓ _____ **SUBORDINATE CLAUSES** [11]
   Incorrect clause formation; poor relationship to main sentence; <u>incorrect subordinator</u>

_____ **RELATIVE CLAUSES** [11]
   Incorrect clause formation; poor relationship to modified noun; incorrect relative pronoun

_____ **HALF-SENTENCES** (Participial Phrases, Absolute Phrases) [12]
   Incorrect formation; poor relationship to main sentence; different subjects

_____ **NOMINAL CLAUSES OR PHRASES** [13]
   Incorrect clause formation; incorrect introducer or substitutor; poor relationship; -*ing*/*to* + base form misuse/confusion

_____ **PASSIVE TRANSFORMATION** [9:1]
   Used inappropriately; incorrect formation

_____ **INDIRECT OBJECT TRANSFORMATION** [9:2]
   Used inappropriately; incorrect formation

_____ **TRANSITION WORDS** [15:1]
   Not used when called for; used inappropriately; poor or incorrect choice

_____ **VARIETY IN WRITING** [7, 12:7, and 15:2]
   Insufficient variety of basic sentence patterns; insufficient variety of combining methods

_____ ✓ _____ **COMMAS** [7:3, 10, 11, 12, 14]
   Incorrect use with shifters; comma splice; incorrect use with relative clauses; incorrect use with half-sentences; incorrect use with (non-restrictive) added information

_____ **VOCABULARY** [All Chapters]
   Too limited; incorrect word choice

_____ ✓✓ _____ **PREPOSITIONS** [*Dyad Learning Program: Prepositions*]
   Incorrect choice; omitted when needed; unnecessarily used

_____ ✓✓ _____ Spelling ✓✓ Capitalization

ESSAY #2

English Second Language

Briefly explain how you studied English before you came here. Then, explain how you plan to study English now. Finally, point out some of the differences and similarities between your two methods of studying English.

In my country we [verb omitted] English schools in many places. In [preposition incorrect] one of them I am studying [verb agreement with time]. In the beginning they teach [article omitted] basic [noun s/p] of English. In the middle school they start teaching grammer [spelling]. Every day we have [verb-time] regular English class. Even though [incomplete] we have [verb-time] our own native language. We [aux omitted] suppose [verb form] to speak [sentence--subordinate clause used alone] English, because [preposition omitted] my country we go [vocabulary incorrect word] more [vocabulary] language [noun s/p].

There are [verb-time] different ways how I study [verb-time] English before I come [verb-time] to [preposition unnecessary] here. Actually [transition word inappropriate], I read books in different [preposition incorrect] kind [noun s/p, word order] at home. [expletive unnecessarily used and basic sentence structure] Every Friday night I go [verb-time] and see [verb-time] movies with the subscription [vocabulary incorrect word] to improve my reading rate.

These are the differences and similarity [noun s/p] of the two methods mention [modifier--incorrect form] above. First [transition word inappropriate], I did not have a friend who speak [verb-time] English as [article or possessive omitted] first language but now I do have [verb unnecessary--compounding incorrect]. I did not have the proper material but now I do have [verb unnecessary--compounding incorrect]. Its [pronoun or article] similarity is that every class discussion was conducted in English and now at this University every thing is conducted in English [compounding incorrect-- unnecessary repetition]. Coming to a country having native language English [clause formation incorrect], I hope I can learn English more easily. I enjoy learn [nominal phrase-- -ing/base form of verb] new language.

Diagnostic/Referral Checklist

_____	**WORD DERIVATIONS** (Forms of Content Words) [1] Noun, verb, adjective, and adverb form confusion/misuse
✓✓✓	**ARTICLES** [2 and *Dyad Learning Program: Determiners*] Incorrect choice; unnecessarily used; <u>omitted when needed</u>
✓✓✓	**NOUNS** [2] <u>Singular-plural</u> or count-noncount confusion/misuse; failure to use proper unit expression with noncount noun
✓	**PRONOUNS** [3 and *Dyad Learning Program: Pronouns*] Lack of agreement with antecedent; <u>ambiguous antecedent</u>; no antecedent; unnecessarily used; not used when called for; incorrect form
✓	**AUXILIARIES AND MODALS** (Aux-words) [4] Incorrect choice; <u>omitted when needed</u>; unnecessarily used
✓✓	**VERB FORMS** [5, 7, and *Dyad Learning Program: Verb Forms and Verb Choices*] <u>Incorrect form</u> (base, *d-t-n*, *-ing* *+s*, no-*s*, past); incorrect verb choice; unnecessarily used; omitted when needed; incorrect use of two-word verbs
_____	**VERB/AUX-AGREEMENT WITH SUBJECT** (Harmony, Concord) [4, 5, 8:1 and *Dyad Learning Program: Verb Forms*] +*s*/no-*s* confusion; ignorance of true nucleus of noun phrase
✓✓✓✓✓✓✓	**VERB/AUX-AGREEMENT WITH TIME** [6 and 13:6] <u>Lack of agreement with general context</u>, with time signal, with other verbs, in complete sentences, and/or with compound noun clauses
✓	**MODIFIERS** [8] <u>Incorrect form</u> (*-ing/d-t-n*, adjective/adverb, etc.); incorrect order; incorrect position in sentence
_____	**COMPARATIVES AND SUPERLATIVES** [8:7, 8:8] Inappropriate comparison; incorrect comparative formation, inappropriate superlative; incorrect superlative formation
✓✓	**BASIC SENTENCE STRUCTURE** [7] <u>Incorrect syntax (word order)</u>; incorrect shifter; omitted object with transitive verb
✓	**EXPLETIVES** *there* or *it* (Dummy Subjects) [3:4, 13] <u>Unnecessarily used</u>; omitted when needed; followed by incorrect form of verb/aux-word
✓	**INCOMPLETE SENTENCES** (Fragments) [7, 8, 11, and 12] Omission of subject; omission of verb; prepositional phrase used alone; <u>subordinate clause used alone</u>; noun phrase used alone; half-sentence used alone
✓✓✓	**COORDINATION** (Compounding) [10] Run-on sentences; comma splice; faulty parallelism, incorrect conjunction choice; <u>incorrect compounding method</u>; <u>unnecessary repetition</u>
_____	**SUBORDINATE CLAUSES** [11] Incorrect clause formation; poor relationship to main sentence; incorrect subordinator
✓	**RELATIVE CLAUSES** [11] <u>Incorrect clause formation</u>; poor relationship to modified noun; incorrect relative pronoun
_____	**HALF-SENTENCES** (Participial Phrases, Absolute Phrases) [12] Incorrect formation; poor relationship to main sentence; different subjects
✓	**NOMINAL CLAUSES OR PHRASES** [13] Incorrect clause formation; incorrect introducer or substitutor; poor relationship; <u>-*ing*/*to*</u> + <u>base form</u> misuse/confusion
_____	**PASSIVE TRANSFORMATION** [9:1] Used inappropriately; incorrect formation
_____	**INDIRECT OBJECT TRANSFORMATION** [9:2] Used inappropriately; incorrect formation
✓✓	**TRANSITION WORDS** [15:1] Not used when called for; <u>used inappropriately</u>; poor or incorrect choice
_____	**VARIETY IN WRITING** [7, 12:7, and 15:2] Insufficient variety of basic sentence patterns; insufficient variety of combining methods
_____	**COMMAS** [7:3, 10, 11, 12, 14] Incorrect use with shifters; comma splice; incorrect use with relative clauses; incorrect use with half-sentences; incorrect use with (non-restrictive) added information
✓✓✓	**VOCABULARY** [All Chapters] Too limited; <u>incorrect word choice</u>
✓✓✓	**PREPOSITIONS** [*Dyad Learning Program: Prepositions*] Incorrect choice; <u>omitted when needed</u>; unnecessarily used
✓	*Spelling*

ESSAY #3

Native Speaker (non-standard dialect)

Why are you at the university? Exactly what do you hope to accomplish while you are here, and how do you plan to accomplish it?

I come to college because I knew it [aux omitted] be a great experience. I wanted to meet people from other place [noun s/p] to see what their life [noun s/p] were compare [modifier—incorrect form] to mine. I wanted to learn some of their traditions, beliefs, etc. I just like meet people and make [nominal phrase—ing/to+base form of verb] friend [noun s/p] with people from all over. I planned ["to" omitted] do this by just mingling with them on and off campus. Also by participating in as many extra curricular activities as I can with them. [incomplete sentence—half-sentence used alone] I came here because I knew that it was a good school academic [word derivation or modifier position]. The teachers here are of the finest quality and compares [verb agreement w/subject] with any other faculties [noun count/noncount] in the nation. Another reason I came here is because I plan to move here after I finish college. Attending [half-sentence—different subjects] school at the University and environment [article omitted] around here, it help [verb agreement with subject] familiarize me more with the area. In my first couple [pronoun agreement] [preposition omitted] years at the University I hope to establish a major in business or physical education or elementary education [compounding incorrect]. By taking [preposition unnecessary] certain classes in these areas and also fulfill [compounding incorrect—faulty parallelism] my own personal goals should help me to choose a definite major.

Diagnostic/Referral Checklist

_____	✓	**WORD DERIVATIONS** (Forms of Content Words) [1]
		Noun, verb, adjective, and <u>adverb</u> form confusion/misuse
_____	✓	**ARTICLES** [2 and *Dyad Learning Program: Determiners*]
		Incorrect choice; unnecessarily used; <u>omitted when needed</u>
_____	✓✓✓✓	**NOUNS** [2]
		Singular-plural or count-noncount confusion/misuse; failure to use proper unit expression with noncount noun
_____	✓	**PRONOUNS** [3 and *Dyad Learning Program: Pronouns*]
		<u>Lack of agreement with antecedent</u>; ambiguous antecedent; no antecedent; unnecessarily used; not used when called for; incorrect form
_____	✓	**AUXILIARIES AND MODALS** (Aux-words) [4]
		Incorrect choice; <u>omitted when needed</u>; unnecessarily used
_____		**VERB FORMS** [5, 7, and *Dyad Learning Program: Verb Forms and Verb Choices*]
		Incorrect form (base, *d-t-n*, *-ing* +*s*, no-*s*, past); incorrect verb choice; unnecessarily used; omitted when needed; incorrect use of two-word verbs
_____	✓✓	**VERB/AUX-AGREEMENT WITH SUBJECT** (Harmony, Concord) [4, 5, 8:1 and *Dyad Learning Program: Verb Forms*]
		+*s*/no-*s* confusion; <u>ignorance of true nucleus of noun phrase</u>
_____		**VERB/AUX-AGREEMENT WITH TIME** [6 and 13:6]
		Lack of agreement with general context, with time signal, with other verbs, in complete sentences, and/or with compound noun clauses
_____	✓✓	**MODIFIERS** [8]
		<u>Incorrect form</u> (*-ing/d-t-n*, adjective/adverb, etc.); incorrect order; <u>incorrect position in sentence</u>
_____		**COMPARATIVES AND SUPERLATIVES** [8:7, 8:8]
		Inappropriate comparison; incorrect comparative formation, inappropriate superlative; incorrect superlative formation
_____		**BASIC SENTENCE STRUCTURE** [7]
		Incorrect syntax (word order); incorrect shifter; omitted object with transitive verb
_____		**EXPLETIVES** *there* or *it* (Dummy Subjects) [3:4, 13]
		Unnecessarily used; omitted when needed; followed by incorrect form of verb/aux-word
_____	✓	**INCOMPLETE SENTENCES** (Fragments) [7, 8, 11, and 12]
		Omission of subject; omission of verb; prepositional phrase used alone; subordinate clause used alone; noun phrase used alone; <u>half-sentence used alone</u>
_____	✓✓	**COORDINATION** (Compounding) [10]
		Run-on sentences; comma splice; <u>faulty parallelism</u>, incorrect conjunction choice; incorrect compounding method; unnecessary repetition
_____		**SUBORDINATE CLAUSES** [11]
		Incorrect clause formation; poor relationship to main sentence; incorrect subordinator
_____		**RELATIVE CLAUSES** [11]
		Incorrect clause formation; poor relationship to modified noun; incorrect relative pronoun
_____	✓	**HALF-SENTENCES** (Participial Phrases, Absolute Phrases) [12]
		Incorrect formation; poor relationship to main sentence; different subjects
_____	✓	**NOMINAL CLAUSES OR PHRASES** [13]
		Incorrect clause formation; incorrect introducer or substitutor; poor relationship; *-ing/to* + base form misuse/confusion
_____		**PASSIVE TRANSFORMATION** [9:1]
		Used inappropriately; incorrect formation
_____		**INDIRECT OBJECT TRANSFORMATION** [9:2]
		Used inappropriately; incorrect formation
_____		**TRANSITION WORDS** [15:1]
		Not used when called for; used inappropriately; poor or incorrect choice
_____		**VARIETY IN WRITING** [7, 12:7, and 15:2]
		Insufficient variety of basic sentence patterns; insufficient variety of combining methods
_____		**COMMAS** [7:3, 10, 11, 12, 14]
		Incorrect use with shifters; comma splice; incorrect use with relative clauses; incorrect use with half-sentences; incorrect use with (non-restrictive) added information
_____		**VOCABULARY** [All Chapters]
		Too limited; incorrect word choice
_____	✓✓	**PREPOSITIONS** [*Dyad Learning Program: Prepositions*]
		Incorrect choice; <u>omitted when needed</u>; unnecessarily used
_____		**OTHER PROBLEMS**

ESSAY #4

Native Speaker (non-standard dialect)

Why are you at the university? Exactly what do you hope to accomplish while you are here, and how do you plan to accomplish it?

I have always wanted to attended [verb form incorrect] a college. I have planned to attend for quite some time. In preparing and making my future a more pleasant and successful one. [incomplete sentence—half-sentence used alone] I hope to be able to receive [basic sentence structure object omitted] in earning a degree in the field of office management. I hope that I will be able to learn the different type [noun s/p] of cultural [word derivation] and the ways of life that is set for them [verb/aux agreement with subject]. I hope that by attending College [preposition incorrect] that [nominal clause formation incorrect—introducer repeated] people will accept me and help [vocabulary—incorrect word] the fact that, [comma unnecessary] we as student [noun s/p] have something in common. I hope also to be able to learn alot [spelling] more interesting things [comparison incorrect] in the various clubs and in [preposition incorrect] getting involve [modifier incorrect form] in all sorts of activities the university has to offered [verb form incorrect] us. And finally, [comma omitted] having these [pronoun—ambiguous antecedent] all adds up to improving myself as a person in trying to prepare future [preposition and article omitted]. Having to set goals, it makes me realize [half sentence—different subjects] how wonderful it is to be a student and going [compounding—faulty parallelism] to a school that can really help me alot [spelling]. The accomplishment [vocabulary—incorrect word] that I have is to strive for the best. In picking and choosing the right decision for myself and my family. [incomplete sentence—half-sentence used alone]

Diagnostic/Referral Checklist

_____   ✓   **WORD DERIVATIONS** (Forms of Content Words) [1]
    <u>Noun</u>, verb, <u>adjective</u>, and adverb form confusion/misuse

_____   ✓   **ARTICLES** [2 and *Dyad Learning Program: Determiners*]
    Incorrect choice; unnecessarily used; <u>omitted when needed</u>

_____   ✓✓   **NOUNS** [2]
    <u>Singular-plural</u> or count-noncount confusion/misuse; failure to use proper unit expression with noncount noun

_____   ✓   **PRONOUNS** [3 and *Dyad Learning Program: Pronouns*]
    Lack of agreement with antecedent; <u>ambiguous antecedent</u>; no antecedent; unnecessarily used; not used when called for; incorrect form

_____   **AUXILIARIES AND MODALS** (Aux-words) [4]
    Incorrect choice; omitted when needed; unnecessarily used

_____   ✓✓   **VERB FORMS** [5, 7, and *Dyad Learning Program: Verb Forms and Verb Choices*]
    Incorrect form (base, *d-t-n*, *-ing* +*s*, no-*s*, past); incorrect verb choice; unnecessarily used; omitted when needed; incorrect use of two-word verbs

_____   ✓   **VERB/AUX-AGREEMENT WITH SUBJECT** (Harmony, Concord) [4, 5, 8:1 and *Dyad Learning Program: Verb Forms*]
    +*s*/no-*s* confusion; ignorance of true nucleus of noun phrase

_____   **VERB/AUX-AGREEMENT WITH TIME** [6 and 13:6]
    Lack of agreement with general context, with time signal, with other verbs, in complete sentences, and/or with compound noun clauses

_____   ✓   **MODIFIERS** [8]
    <u>Incorrect form</u> (-*ing*/*d-t-n*, adjective/adverb, etc.); incorrect order; incorrect position in sentence

_____   ✓   **COMPARATIVES AND SUPERLATIVES** [8:7, 8:8]
    Inappropriate comparison; <u>incorrect comparative formation</u>, inappropriate superlative; incorrect superlative formation

_____   ✓   **BASIC SENTENCE STRUCTURE** [7]
    Incorrect syntax (word order); <u>incorrect shifter</u>; <u>omitted object with transitive verb</u>

_____   **EXPLETIVES** *there* or *it* (Dummy Subjects) [3:4, 13]
    Unnecessarily used; omitted when needed; followed by incorrect form of verb/aux-word

_____   ✓✓   **INCOMPLETE SENTENCES** (Fragments) [7, 8, 11, and 12]
    Omission of subject; omission of verb; prepositional phrase used alone; subordinate clause used alone; noun phrase used alone; <u>half-sentence used alone</u>

_____   ✓   **COORDINATION** (Compounding) [10]
    Run-on sentences; comma splice; <u>faulty parallelism</u>, incorrect conjunction choice; incorrect compounding method; unnecessary repetition

_____   **SUBORDINATE CLAUSES** [11]
    Incorrect clause formation; poor relationship to main sentence; incorrect subordinator

_____   **RELATIVE CLAUSES** [11]
    Incorrect clause formation; poor relationship to modified noun; incorrect relative pronoun

_____   ✓   **HALF-SENTENCES** (Participial Phrases, Absolute Phrases) [12]
    Incorrect formation; poor relationship to main sentence; <u>different subjects</u>

_____   ✓   **NOMINAL CLAUSES OR PHRASES** [13]
    <u>Incorrect clause formation</u>; incorrect introducer or substitutor; poor relationship; -*ing*/*to* + base form misuse/confusion

_____   **PASSIVE TRANSFORMATION** [9:1]
    Used inappropriately; incorrect formation

_____   **INDIRECT OBJECT TRANSFORMATION** [9:2]
    Used inappropriately; incorrect formation

_____   **TRANSITION WORDS** [15:1]
    Not used when called for; used inappropriately; poor or incorrect choice

_____   **VARIETY IN WRITING** [7, 12:7, and 15:2]
    Insufficient variety of basic sentence patterns; insufficient variety of combining methods

_____   ✓✓   **COMMAS** [7:3, 10, 11, 12, 14]
    <u>Incorrect use with shifters</u>; comma splice; incorrect use with relative clauses; incorrect use with half-sentences; incorrect use with (non-restrictive) added information

_____   ✓✓   **VOCABULARY** [All Chapters]
    Too limited; <u>incorrect word choice</u>

_____   ✓✓✓   **PREPOSITIONS** [*Dyad Learning Program: Prepositions*]
    <u>Incorrect choice</u>; <u>omitted when needed</u>; unnecessarily used

_____   ✓✓   *Spelling*

SENTENCE CONSTRUCTION
Writing and Combining Standard English Sentences

Book I

1
WORD TYPES AND FORMS

1. CONTENT AND FUNCTION WORDS

In English there are two types of words:
(1) content words, and (2) function words.

Examples:

Content Words	Function Words
book	a
diesel	the
archaeology	of
read	and
elephant	or
typewriter	not
quickly	when
horrible	about
man	under

The number of function words is very small (about 150) when compared with the large number of content words (thousands and continually increasing), but function words are used very frequently and must be used precisely in written English. You are not expected to know all the content words in English (nobody does), but you must understand and use all the function words.

The following sentences show how content and function words are used.

    The man quickly read a book about archaeology.
     F   C   C   C F C   F   C

    Clark has studied the history of the Egyptian pyramids.
     C   F   C   F   C   F F   C   C

Read all five sentences below. Then copy them. Put a C beneath each content word and an F beneath each function word.

1. Each language has its own content and function words.
2. Content words seem to represent some thing or concept.
3. Function words show the relationship between the content words.
4. The function of these words must be learned.
5. The function words in different languages do not have meanings that translate directly.

2   SENTENCE CONSTRUCTION

2. CONTENT WORDS AND DERIVATIONAL CLASSES

2.1   There are four classes of content words:

Examples:
>   Nouns: John, pencil, soap, air, mountain
>   Verbs: jump, think, read, go, remember
>   Adjectives: pretty, wild, hungry, blue, triangular
>   Adverbs: quickly, seriously, often, never, happily

A content word in one class usually has related forms in other classes. All these related forms make up a word family.

Some word families have forms in all four classes. Others do not. Occasionally different forms of content words may be spelled the same way.

2.2   Because all word families do not have forms in all classes, some words can only be used in certain sentence positions.

Example:
>   A *grateful* (adjective) man may show his *gratitude* (noun) by thanking someone *gratefully* (adverb).

(In English there is no verb form to express this idea of being grateful or showing gratitude.)

2.3   Sometimes there is more than one form in each class (see *circle* and *employ* in the list below). Sometimes the meanings of these different forms are very close (e.g., *circle* and *encircle*), but sometimes they are quite different (e.g., *employee, employer,* and *employment*).

Examples:

Noun	Verb	Adjective	Adverb
beauty	beautify	beautiful	beautifully
vacancy	vacate	vacant	vacantly
jealousy	(no verb form)	jealous	jealously
qualification	qualify	qualified	(no adverb form)
work	work	working	(no adverb form)
circle	circle encircle	circular circled circling	circularly
employment employee employer	employ	employed employable	(no adverb form)

A larger list of the forms of content words is found in Appendix A, page 149.

2.4   Some nouns and certain forms (d-t-n and -ing) of some verbs may be used as adjectives. The use of these forms is explained in Chapter 8. When used as modifiers, they are classified as adjectives although they have noun or verb forms.

Example:
>   The *working* man ate his *box* lunch.
>   verb form as adj.   noun form as adj.

Assignment 2:A

Find the different forms of the following content words in the passage below. On your paper write the number of each sentence. After the number, write the different forms you find.

history   build   early   discover

ANCIENT AMERICAN RUINS

[1] No one knows the real history of the pyramids built in Mexico and Guatemala in earlier days, or who their builders were. [2] Many of these historic buildings were completely destroyed by the early Spaniards. [3] Christian churches were built on the sites of earlier Mayan and Toltec places of worship. [4] Historians state that later civilizations built upon the foundations of earlier buildings, even before the Spaniards came. [5] Many of the earlier discovered ruins have been rebuilt, and tourists come to see these historic buildings. [6] In Mexico City, workers, building a new subway, discovered unknown ruins from an earlier civilization. [7] When they started to build the Olympic Village, once again remnants of an early civilization were uncovered. [8] Historically, the discovery of any ancient ruin is a significant find, and historians and archaeologists are thrilled to discover one.

Assignment 2:B

Find the different forms of the following content words in the passage below. On your paper write the number of each sentence. After the number, write the different forms you find.

flower   tropical   beauty   produce   brief

FLOWERING TREES

[1] Flowering trees are often found in the tropics. [2] These trees produce beautiful flowers all year but do not bear edible fruit. [3] Their only valuable products are beauty and shade. [4] Their beautifully colored flowers are in contrast to the green which is seen everywhere in tropical climates.

[5] In other, non-tropical parts of the world, the only flowers trees produce are blossoms which beautify the environment just once a year. [6] The beauty of these blossoms lasts only a brief time but is often appreciated more because of its brevity. [7] This short period of beauty is often followed by another longer period of productivity during which fruit is produced.

Assignment 2:C

Find the different forms of the following content words in the passage below. On your paper write the number of each sentence. After the number, write the different forms you find.

know   education   important   communicate

FOREIGN LANGUAGE STUDY

[1] The knowledge of a foreign language is an important part of an education. [2] A person cannot be considered truly educated if he knows only one language. [3] Nevertheless, the importance of learning foreign languages is often underestimated.

[4] English is one of the most commonly used languages in international communication. [5] Some speakers of English mistakenly argue that it is unimportant for them to know another language for communicative purposes. [6] They think that everyone else should know English. [7] But there are still billions of people who do not speak English, and many of these people have limited educational opportunities. [8] If English speakers do not make the effort to learn to communicate in other languages, they should not expect others to gain a knowledge of English.

[9] If there is to be world peace, the people of the world must understand each other. [10] Communication is necessary to that understanding, but people cannot communicate if they do not speak the same language.

4 SENTENCE CONSTRUCTION

3. CONTENT WORDS AND INFLECTIONAL FORMS

3.1 All of the four classes of content words except the adverb class have a number of forms. Nouns may be singular or plural (this is explained in Chapter 2), each verb has six forms (this is explained in Chapter 5), and adjectives often have comparative and superlative forms (this is explained in Chapter 8).

Examples:

Noun	Verb		Adjective	Adverb
	Timeless	Time Included		
anger	anger	angers	angry	angrily
(noncount)	angered	anger	angrier	
	angering	angered	(the) angriest	
civilization	civilize	civilizes	civilized	(no adverb
civilizations	civilized	civilize	(more) civilized	form)
(count)	civilizing	civilized	(the most) civilized	
kindness			kind	kindly
kindliness	(no verb form)			
(noncount)				
tolerance	tolerate	tolerates	tolerable	tolerably
toleration	tolerated	tolerate	(more) tolerable	
(noncount)	tolerating	tolerated	(the most) tolerable	
			(more) tolerant	
			(the most) tolerant	
action	act	acts	active	actively
actions	acted	act	(more) active	
act	acting	acted	(the most) active	
acts				
actor				
actors				
actress				
actresses				
(count)				
ability	enable	enables	able	ably
abilities	enabled	enable	abler	
(count and noncount)	enabling	enabled	(the) ablest	

3.2 You will notice in the above chart that the differences between the forms of each class are created by changes at the ends of the words. Other changes can be made at the front of some words by adding a prefix. However, the addition of a prefix changes the meaning of the word, and not the way it is used in a sentence.

Examples:
    pre- (= before)
        preview, prehistoric, preheat
    re- (= again)
        replay, rewrite, redecorate
    un- (= negative)
        unusual, unkind, unnatural

There are many prefixes in English. The ones above are only examples. Prefixes and their meanings can be found in a good dictionary.

Some prefixes have more than one meaning (e.g., *un-* used with a verb means a *reversal* of the action, not its *negative*).

Sometimes one meaning is expressed by several different prefixes (e.g., *non-*, *un-*, *ir-*, *in-*, *im-*, and *mis-* all form the negative of the word they are added to). Words usually require a particular prefix for a meaning and care must be taken to use the correct prefix. (e.g., The prefix *im-* is the only negative prefix that can be used with the word *possible*. Similarly, if a negative meaning of the word *regular* is desired, only the prefix *ir-* can be added.)

Assignment 3:A

Find the different forms of the following content words in the passage below. On your paper write the number of each sentence. After the number, write the different forms you find. Also write NOUN after the noun forms, VERB after the verb forms, ADJ after the adjective forms, and ADV after the adverb forms of the words you write.

history   discover   migrate   America

EARLY AMERICANS

[1]Historians would like to discover the origin of the American Indian, whose history is unknown. [2]Migration theories suggest origins in Asia, Egypt, or India. [3]Recorded history tells us that there were people living in America when Columbus discovered it. [4]Unlike the Polynesians, whose historical chants tell how their ancestors came in great canoes, the American Indians have no historic accounts of migration. [5]However, ruins built upon earlier ruins have been discovered which show that people did migrate to or within America. [6]The discovery of old buildings and artifacts sheds light on earlier civilizataions and their migrations. [7]Historians continue to work with archeologists to discover new facts about ancient American people and their migrations.

Assignment 3:B

Find the different forms of the following content words in the passage below. On your paper write the number of each sentence. After the number, write the different forms you find. Also write NOUN after the noun forms, VERB after the verb forms, ADJ after the adjective forms, and ADV after the adverb forms of the words you write.

beautiful   art   paint

ART

[1]Most of us appreciate art and admire a beautiful painting. [2]We wish we were artists and could paint a thing of beauty too. [3]What we fail to realize is the time the artist spends in preparation. [4]An artist spends hundreds of hours in art classes and invests hundreds of dollars in painting supplies before he can create a masterpiece. [5]Artistic talent is not enough; a talented person must develop his natural gift. [6]One is not a real artist until he has learned to make his brush and paints express artistically the beauty he sees around him.

[7]Writing is also an art. [8]Beautiful writing, like beautiful painting, involves an investment in time and energy. [9]Even talented writers must write and rewrite before their writing is artistically satisfying to both writer and reader.

Assignment 3:C

Find the different forms of the following content words in the passage below. On your paper write the number of each sentence. After the number, write the different forms you find. Also write NOUN after the noun forms, VERB after the verb forms, ADJ after the adjective forms, and ADV after the adverb forms of the words you write.

tax **reduce** **donate** **deduct**

TAXES

[1]Taxation is an inescapable part of modern life. [2]People must pay taxes on nearly everything. [3]They are taxed when they make money and taxed when they spend money. [4]They also pay taxes on things they own. [5]The federal government taxes people, and state and local governments also levy taxes. [6]People often do things to reduce their taxes. [7]To increase their deductions they make charitable donations, political contributions, and keep careful records of their deductible expenditures.

[8]Money donated to worthy causes benefits both the donor and the organization which receives the donation. [9]Many organizations depend on donors for much of their support, and donating money often reduces the taxpayer's taxable income, resulting in tax reductions.

[10]Sometimes people get in trouble by listing illegal deductions. [11]There are stiff penalties for tax evasion. [12]People should donate money to worthy causes and avoid paying more taxes than necessary, but they must not evade the payment of taxes they owe.

Assignment 3.1:A

Here are some words. Write all the forms of each one in table form (as indicated). Then, rewrite the sentences below filling in the blanks with the correct forms (noun, verb, adjective, and adverb) of these words.

Noun	Verb	Adjective	Adverb
student			
		different	
culture			
			friendly

Note: There may be more than one correct answer for each blank. Choose the one you think is best.

CULTURAL SHOCK

[1]When they go away to school, many _____ experience _____ shock. [2]The language is _____. [3]There are other _____ too. [4]The food is cooked _____.

[5]Every _____ has its own ways of being _____ — some are quiet, others are noisy.

[6]A _____ misses family and _____ at home. [7]Although many students are very _____ and work hard, they can't _____ all the time. [8]As they become accustomed

to the new _____, students experience less _____ shock. ⁹When they make new _____, things don't seem as _____ as they used to. ¹⁰Often when they return home, _____ have to adapt to _____ in their former _____ and once again suffer from _____ shock.

Assignment 3.1:B

Here are some words. Write all the forms of each one in table form (as indicated). Then, rewrite the sentences below filling in the blanks with the correct forms (noun, verb, adjective, and adverb) of these words.

Noun	Verb	Adjective	Adverb
intelligence			
	compute		
			capably
		complex	
emotion			

Note: There may be more than one correct answer for each blank. Choose the one you think is best.

COMPUTERS

¹_____ form an important part of our _____ modern civilization. ²Our _____ world frightens some people. ³They fear _____ because they think an "electronic brain" must be extremely _____. ⁴Others reply that an "electronic brain" has no real _____, it can only _____. ⁵Today, although _____ can beat champion chess players, they are not _____ or _____. ⁶They have no _____, only memories. ⁷_____ are growing more and more _____. ⁸As their _____ grows, so will their _____. ⁹Someday _____ may be programmed to react _____. ¹⁰Then they may be _____ of human _____. ¹¹Perhaps then _____ will have _____ as well as electronic breakdowns.

SENTENCE CONSTRUCTION

Assignment 3.1:C

Here are some words. Write all the forms of each one in table form (as indicated). Then, rewrite the sentences below filling in the blanks with the correct forms (noun, verb, adjective, and adverb) of these words.

Noun	Verb	Adjective	Adverb
comfort			
		foreign	
	notice		
			strangely

Note: There may be more than one correct answer for each blank. Choose the one you think is best.

CULTURAL ADJUSTMENT

[1] When people travel to _____ countries, they often do _____ things. [2] They don't realize that they, not the people around them, are the _____ . [3] The _____ of their actions is not always _____ to them. [4] They don't understand why the local people look at them _____ . [5] If they don't speak the local language, everything sounds _____ to them. [6] They begin to feel very un_____ . [7] Frustrated by the _____ of the new environment, they retreat to the _____ of things from their own country. [8] They associate only with their fellow countrymen and _____ each other. [9] They avoid eating foods that are _____ different. [10] Sometimes they never become _____ with the local customs. [11] Then they return home impressed only by the _____ of people in _____ lands.

2
NOUNS

1. TYPES OF NOUNS

1.1 English nouns are divided into four main groups:

1. **count nouns**—which have singular and plural forms,*
2. **noncount nouns**—which do not have plural forms,
3. **group (or collective) nouns**—which have only one form, but may be singular or plural, and
4. **proper nouns**—names which are capitalized.

Count Nouns		Noncount Nouns	Group Nouns	Proper Nouns
Singular	Plural			
banana	bananas	bacon	class	Christmas
class	classes	chalk	committee	John
gallon	gallons	furniture	faculty	London
hamburger	hamburgers	hamburger	herd	Mars
instructor	instructors	homework	jury	Mr. Jones
library	libraries	ink	majority	Mt. Whitney
mile	miles	material	minority	Pennsylvania Turnpike
pencil	pencils	paper	orchestra	
sheep	sheep	pressure	police	
student	students	rice	team	
suitcase	suitcases	tuition		
team	teams	water		
wheel	wheels	wax		

A longer list of noncount nouns and their unit expressions is found in Appendix B, page 153.

Group nouns are followed by singular verb forms when the entire group acts as a unit. Group nouns are plural when each part acts individually.

Examples:
>   The jury has reached a verdict.
>   The jury are arguing among themselves.

*There are a few count nouns which do not have singular forms, such as *cattle* and *people*.

SENTENCE CONSTRUCTION

1.2 When asking or answering questions about quantity, you must know if the noun is a count or noncount noun.

How many is used with count nouns.
How much is used with noncount nouns.

Examples:

How many bananas do you want?	(count noun)
How much rice do you want?	(noncount noun)
How many suitcases do you have?	(count noun)
How much homework do you have?	(noncount noun)
How many armies fought in the war?	(group noun)

Note that in asking *how many* the count noun used is plural.

1.3 Some nouns can either be count or noncount, depending on the meaning.

Examples:

He ate five hamburgers yesterday. (count noun)
He bought five pounds of hamburger yesterday. (noncount noun)
She wants her hamburger without catsup. (count noun)
She uses hamburger to make meat loaf. (noncount noun)
I saw a film at the Paramount Theatre yesterday. (count noun)
I need some film for my camera. (noncount noun)

1.4 Noncount nouns become count nouns when they are used to indicate classes or species.

Examples:

the fruits of the Northwest (apples, cherries, pears, etc.)
the teas of China (black tea, green tea, etc.)
the foods of Hawaii (pineapple, poi, taro, breadfruit, etc.)

Assignment 1:A

Write the following questions using How much *or* How many, *whichever is appropriate, in place of the blanks.*

THIS CLASS

1. _____ students are there in this class?

2. _____ homework do you have to do?

3. _____ books do you need to buy?

4. _____ money do they cost?

5. _____ time do you have to spend studying every day?

6. _____ tests are there?

7. _____ students attend this school?

8. _____ nationalities do they represent?

9. _____ languages do they speak?

10. _____ tuition do they have to pay?

11. _____ material do they study?

12. _____ things do they learn?

Assignment 1:B

Write the following questions using How much *or* How many, *whichever is appropriate, in place of the blanks.*

YOUR CAR

1. _____ money did you pay for this car?

2. _____ years have you owned it?

3. _____ miles have you driven it?

4. _____ gas is in the gas tank?

5. _____ gallons of gas did you buy yesterday?

6. _____ cylinders does it have?

7. _____ carburetors does it have?

8. _____ power does it have?

9. _____ water did you put in the radiator?

10. _____ oil do you have to add every week?

11. _____ air pressure does each tire take?

12. _____ tread is left on each one?

Assignment 1:C

Write the following questions using How much *or* How many, *whichever is appropriate, in place of the blanks.*

THE NEWS

1. _____ news was there on the TV today?

2. _____ people listened to it?

3. _____ coverage was there on sports?

4. _____ minutes did the entire broadcast take?

5. _____ emphasis was given to the weather?

6. _____ advertising was there?

7. _____ different sponsors were there?

12 SENTENCE CONSTRUCTION

8. _____ men were on the news team?

9. _____ women were there?

10. _____ news was international?

11. _____ national news was there?

12. _____ local broadcasters were there?

13. _____ benefit did you gain from listening to the news?

14. _____ time did you waste watching TV today?

2. NOUNS AND UNIT EXPRESSIONS

2.1 **Count nouns** indicate units. To indicate quantity, all that is necessary is a number before the noun.

Examples:
   five bananas
   twenty students

Unit expressions of quantity may also be used with count nouns.

Examples:
   five boxes of pencils
   two crates of oranges

2.2 **Noncount nouns** do **not** indicate units. When referring to quantity, noncount nouns require a unit expression. The number is placed before the unit expression.

Examples:
   five bowls of rice
   three rooms of furniture

When quantity is not being considered, the unit expression is not necessary.

Examples:
   Furniture is expensive.
   Butter contains vitamin A.

Assignment 2:A

The nouns listed below are all noncount nouns. Use appropriate unit expressions in answering the question "What did Mr. and Mrs. Murphy buy?"

Examples:

   soap (3)   They bought three bars of soap.
   milk (2)   They bought two cartons of milk.
   butter (1) They bought a pound of butter.

Assignment 2:A	Assignment 2:B	Assignment 2:C
1. cheese (3)	1. oil (5)	1. rope (3)
2. bacon (1)	2. wax (1)	2. kerosene (1)
3. flour (5)	3. soap (3)	3. chalk (2)
4. sugar (5)	4. ink (1)	4. cleaning fluid (3)
5. cream (3)	5. paper (2)	5. distilled water (1)
6. jam (2)	6. paste (1)	6. baking soda (1)
7. honey (1)	7. glue (1)	7. linen (3)
8. cereal (4)	8. glass (4)	8. paper (4)
9. lettuce (2)	9. furniture (3)	9. chalk (3)
10. hamburger (5)	10. leather (5)	10. masking tape (2)
11. ice cream (3)	11. cloth (6)	11. detergent (2)
12. rice (5)	12. furniture polish (2)	12. aluminum foil (4)

3. ARTICLES AND NOUNS (NONSPECIFIC)

3.1 Function words called articles (*a/an, the*) often come before nouns (and any modifiers which precede the nouns).

Examples:

> *the* painting on the wall
> *the* blue dress in the window
> *a* large, carved, wooden bowl
> *a* baby elephant
> *an* elephant
> *an* orange

An article must be used before a singular count noun except in the following places:

1. When a possessive (*my, your, his,* etc.) or demonstrative (*this, that, these,* or *those*) is used before a singular count noun, no article is used.
2. When words like *school, jail, prison, church,* or *town* are preceded by prepositions (such as *to, in,* or *at*), generally no article is used.
3. When making a general statement about a count noun, the plural is generally used. However, in a few cases, the singular form may be used. In either case, no article is needed.

Examples:

> Bananas are my favorite fruit.
> Porpoises seem almost human.
> Men are the most intelligent creatures on earth. or,
> Man is the most intelligent creature on earth.

3.2 The article *a/an* is used only with **nonspecific** (unidentified—often called indefinite), singular count nouns.

The *an* form is used before words beginning with **vowel sounds.**
The *a* form is used before words beginning with **consonant sounds.**

Examples:

> a color   an onion
> a tree   an hour
> a university   an encyclopedia
> a man   an honest man
> a big orange   an orange

SENTENCE CONSTRUCTION

3.3 With plural count nouns and noncount nouns, the function word *some* is the most often used nonspecific (indefinite) indicator.

Examples:

    a penny   a man
    some pennies   some men

Assignment 3:A

Write the sentences below, supplying a, an, *or* some, *whichever is appropriate, in place of the blanks.*

LUNCHTIME

[1] Would you like _____ orange? [2] No, but I would like _____ orange juice. [3] I'm sorry. We don't have any orange juice. Would you like _____ coffee? [4] No thank you. I'll just have _____ sandwich. [5] Would you like _____ tomato juice to go with it? [6] No, I just had _____ tomato soup. [7] How about _____ egg? [8] That sounds good, but I think I'll have _____ hot dog instead. [9] After that I want to eat _____ banana or two. [10] I might have _____ milk with the bananas. [11] I would like _____ other fruit also, but I can't see any. [12] To finish off, I will have _____ tea. [13] I'd like _____ sugar in it, but not too much. [14] That was _____ delicious lunch. [15] I need only one more thing, _____ toothpick.

Assignment 3:B

Write the sentences below, supplying a, an, *or* some, *whichever is appropriate, in place of the blanks.*

FRIENDS

[1] Everyone needs _____ friend. [2] _____ true friend is _____ person who remains _____ friend even when _____ difficulty arises. [3] _____ people are "good weather" friends who always want to share _____ good time but are not to be found when _____ unpleasant situation occurs. [4] _____ people are friends with anyone who has _____ money or has _____ power or influence. [5] Are you _____ true friend or, like _____ others, _____ "fair weather" friend?

Assignment 3:C

Write the sentences below, supplying a, an, *or* some, *whichever is appropriate, in place of the blanks.*

GAINING KNOWLEDGE

¹_____ students feel they need _____ reason to read _____ book.

²Unless _____ teacher makes _____ assignment to read _____ specific chapter, the students do not look at even _____ page of the text. ³Although _____ instruction is given orally, unless _____ student does _____ reading from the text and _____ research in outside sources, he will have _____ knowledge of the subject, but it will be limited. ⁴_____ true scholar always seeks _____ additional knowledge on _____ subject. ⁵He thus has _____ better understanding of the subject than _____ of the other students.

4. ARTICLES AND NOUNS (SPECIFIC)

4.1 Nouns may become identified with use. The article used with a noun then changes from *a/an* to *the*.

Examples:
 A small boy is playing a game. *The* boy is my brother.

4.2 A noun is considered specifically identified if

1. it is mentioned earlier (in a previous sentence), or

Examples:
 I can see a fish. I'd like to catch the fish.

2. it is identified later in the same sentence, or

Examples:
 The trophy on the shelf is mine.

3. the situation (context) clearly identifies the noun.

Examples:
 When I got out of bed this morning, I opened the window.
  (the window is in my bedroom)
 At school today, George emptied the wastebasket.
  (the wastebasket at school)

4.3 Certain **adjectives** preceded by *the* are sometimes used to represent the noun group they modify. In such cases, the noun is not used.

Examples:
 Robin Hood robbed *rich people* and gave money to *poor people*.
 Robin Hood robbed *the rich* and gave money to *the poor*.
 The English navy defeated *the Spanish armada*.
 The English defeated *the Spanish*.

16 SENTENCE CONSTRUCTION

Assignment 4:A

Write the following sentences, replacing the blanks with either a, an, *or* the, *whichever is appropriate.*

A TRAFFIC INCIDENT

¹I saw _____ boy walking across the street today. ²_____ boy was almost hit by _____ car. ³_____ car was speeding. ⁴_____ policeman saw what happened. ⁵_____ policeman chased and stopped _____ car. ⁶He gave _____ driver of _____ car _____ ticket. ⁷_____ ticket cost _____ speeding motorist forty-five dollars.

Assignment 4:B

Write the following sentences, replacing the blanks with either a, an, *or* the, *whichever is appropriate.*

THE LION AND THE MOUSE

¹_____ lion was awakened by _____ mouse running across his face. ²With _____ great roar, _____ lion grabbed _____ mouse and was about to kill him. ³"Oh please," _____ mouse begged. "Spare my life! Someday I will repay your kindness." ⁴_____ lion was so amused at _____ thought of _____ small mouse being able to help _____ king of beasts that he let _____ tiny creature go. ⁵Later _____ lion, caught in _____ trap set by some hunters, was hopelessly tangled in _____ net of strong ropes. ⁶_____ lion roared so loudly that all _____ beasts in _____ forest heard him. ⁷_____ mouse recognized _____ roar and ran to _____ place where _____ lion lay trapped. ⁸_____ mouse began to chew _____ rope until at last _____ lion was free. ⁹"Thank you," said _____ lion. ¹⁰"I now see that _____ weak can help _____ strong."

Assignment 4:C

Write the following sentences replacing the blanks with either a, an, *or* the, *whichever is appropriate.*

THE LION AND THE DONKEY

¹_____ donkey and _____ rooster lived together in _____ farmyard. ²One day _____ hungry lion passed by. ³When he saw _____ plump donkey,

he thought of _____ fine meal it would make. ⁴Just as _____ lion was about to pounce on _____ donkey, _____ rooster began to crow. ⁵Now there is nothing _____ lion hates more than _____ sound of _____ rooster's crowing. ⁶_____ lion turned and ran away at _____ sound of _____ *cock-a-doodle-doo*. ⁷_____ donkey laughed. ⁸"Why, _____ lion is _____ coward! ⁹_____ mighty king of beasts runs from _____ rooster." ¹⁰Then _____ donkey felt so bold that he began to chase _____ lion. ¹¹He had not run very far, however, when _____ lion turned and leaped upon _____ donkey. ¹²_____ rooster, watching from _____ farmyard, said sadly, "It's too bad my poor friend did not understand what he could and could not do."

5. EXPRESSIONS OF QUANTITY WITH *A*

5.1 Some expressions of quantity use *a* although they are used with noncount nouns or plural count nouns (which are never used with *a* alone).

Examples:

    a few (count noun plural)
        A few people came to the meeting.
    a little (noncount noun)
        Just use a little sugar.
    a great many (count noun plural)
        A great many people came to the meeting.
    a couple of (count noun plural)
        I'll be ready in a couple of minutes.
    a lot of (either noncount or count noun plural)
        A lot of time is needed to get it ready.
        A lot of people are needed for this play.
    a number of (count noun plural)
        A number of people are waiting to see you.
    a portion of (count noun plural or noncount noun)
        A portion of the delegates are undecided.
        A portion of the water is contaminated.

5.2 The meanings of the phrases *a few* and *a little* are different from the meanings of the single words *few* and *little*. This difference lies in the emphasis or point of view.

Examples:

    A few people came to the meeting. (at least somebody came)
    Few people came to the meeting. (not as many as expected)
    There's little hope for the injured boy. (he'll probably die)
    There's a little hope for the injured boy. (he may live)

6. ARTICLES AND PROPER NOUNS

6.1 *The* is the only article used with **proper** nouns (the names of people, places, institutions, etc.) and it is only used in certain cases.

6.2 When *of* is part of the name, *the* is usually necessary.

Examples:

>   the United States of America   the Bank of America
>   the University of Michigan   (an exception is Lloyds of London)

6.3 *The* is used with the names of **canals, deserts, forests, oceans, rivers,** and **seas**. It is also used when the names of **islands, lakes,** and **mountains** are **plural** but not when they are singular. (See 6.5 below.)

Examples:

>   the Panama Canal   the Dead Sea
>   the Gobi Desert   the Aleutian Islands
>   the Black Forest   the Great Lakes
>   the Pacific Ocean   the Rocky Mountains
>   the Yangtze River

(In some cases the word ocean, sea, river, desert, or mountains can be deleted. For example, *the Pacific, the Caribbean, the Sahara, the Alps.*)

6.4 *The* is used with the names of **libraries** and **museums**. It is also used with the names of **clubs** and **documents**.

Examples:

>   the Carnegie Library   the National Gallery
>   the Metropolitan Museum   the Rotary Club
>   the Mayflower Compact   the Smithsonian Institute

6.5 *The* is **not** used with the names of **parks** or with **singular** names of **islands, lakes, mountains,** or **valleys**.

Examples:

>   Hyde Park   Lake Victoria
>   Pitcairn Island   Mount Rushmore

(an exception is the Great Salt Lake)

6.6 *The* is **not** used with the names of **streets, avenues, boulevards, roads,** and **lanes**, but *the* is used with the names of **turnpikes, freeways,** and **expressways**.

Examples:

>   Main Street   the Pennsylvania Turnpike
>   Pennsylvania Avenue   the Riverside Expressway
>   Ventura Boulevard   the Golden Gate Freeway
>   Canyon Road
>   Sunnybrook Lane

6.7 Some proper nouns must be preceded by *the* while others never use the article.

Examples:

>   Russia   the Soviet Union
>   North Africa   the North Pole
>   Carnegie Hall   the World Trade Center

Nouns

Assignment 6: A

Write the following paragraph, supplying articles (a, an, or the) when needed. In some cases no article is necessary.

A SHORT VACATION

[1] Many people like to travel on holiday _____ weekends. [2] Driving their own _____ cars, they can go as far as they want and stop when they please. [3] _____ nice three or four day trip from _____ Los Angeles, California is to drive up to _____ San Francisco either following _____ Pacific Ocean highway or alternately through _____ San Joaquin Valley. [4] _____ nice side trip from _____ San Francisco is to cross _____ Golden Gate Bridge and drive through _____ redwood forests of _____ Northern California. [5] After _____ return through _____ Sacramento, one can drive by _____ Lake Tahoe and over _____ Donner Pass through _____ Sierra Nevada Mountains. [6] After passing through _____ Reno, _____ route goes through _____ Mojave Desert. [7] If it's _____ summer trip, one should avoid _____ Death Valley and come back over _____ mountains through _____ pass in _____ Sierra Nevadas, crossing _____ California-Nevada border near _____ Baker, California. [8] _____ delightful drive paralleling _____ Los Angeles aqueduct is part of _____ return trip to _____ Los Angeles.

Assignment 6: B

Write the following paragraph, supplying articles (a, an, or the) when needed. In some cases no article is necessary.

A QUICK TRIP AROUND THE WORLD

[1] _____ international airline advertises that one can take _____ trip around _____ world in _____ three days. [2] Some people have actually made this three-day trip. [3] Leaving at _____ Los Angeles, it consists of crossing _____ Pacific Ocean

20   SENTENCE CONSTRUCTION

to _____ Japan with _____ short stop on the Island of Oahu in _____ Hawaii. ⁴This stop is not long enough to visit _____ Waikiki Beach or even see _____ palm tree. ⁵After this brief stop, _____ flight is again over _____ Pacific Ocean without _____ stop in _____ Philippines or on any of _____ islands in _____ Trust Territory. ⁶One cannot stay in _____ Tokyo for _____ night's rest or to see famous _____ Mt. Fuji. ⁷After _____ flight over _____ Taiwan, _____ Hong Kong is _____ next stop. ⁸Then it's over _____ Yellow Sea only seeing _____ Macao and _____ Vietnam from _____ air. ⁹There is _____ short stop in _____ New Delhi (which is in _____ India), but there is no time to visit _____ Taj Mahal in _____ Agra. ¹⁰Then it's on to _____ Beirut for _____ twenty-minute stop and from there to _____ Rome, Italy. ¹¹One can only dream of seeing _____ Vatican, _____ Sistine Chapel, _____ St. Peter's Cathedral and all _____ other beautiful sights in _____ Italy as _____ plane is soon on its way to _____ Paris, France. ¹²Along the way, if it's _____ clear day, one can see _____ Alps in all their snowy splendor. ¹³In _____ Paris, unfortunately, there is no _____ time to see _____ Eiffel Tower and _____ Louvre—probably _____ most famous museum in _____ world.

Assignment 6:C

*Write the following paragraph, supplying articles (*a, an, *or* the*) when needed. In some cases no article is necessary.*

A QUICK TRIP AROUND THE WORLD II

¹On _____ way to _____ London one has not time to see _____ changing of _____ guard, _____ numerous stage productions, _____ Tower of London, or _____ crown jewels as _____ plane is soon on its way back to _____ California. ²If it is _____ clear day, one can see icebergs in _____ North Atlantic Ocean. ³_____ short refueling stop in Iceland is _____ only delay

Nouns 21

on this leg of _____ journey. ⁴_____ daylight flight offers _____ spectacular view of _____ Arctic wastes before crossing _____ Hudson Bay and _____ Canada. ⁵Possibly, heavy _____ clouds may block your view of _____ Rocky Mountains and _____ wheat fields of _____ Saskatchewan, but cramped _____ muscles will welcome _____ soon-to-come end of _____ trip. ⁶_____ weary traveler will probably sleep away _____ twenty-four hours he gained by flying _____ west continually. ⁷Possibly _____ prestige value of being able to say one has been around _____ world is _____ only compensation for _____ cost in _____ time, _____ money, and _____ fatigue to make _____ trip. ⁸One could see much more of _____ world in _____ two-hour travelogue movie.

3
PRONOUNS

1. PURPOSE OF PRONOUNS

Pronouns, though function words, represent nouns (which are content words) or noun phrases. (A chart of English pronouns is found on page 24.)

Pronouns are used to avoid unnecessary repetition of the nouns they represent and to allow variety and brevity in writing.

Read the following paragraphs aloud and note how the use of pronouns improves the second paragraph by reducing repetition.

Rock Festivals

Rock festivals have been extremely popular during the past several years. Rock festivals often last as long as three days. Rock festivals are advertised widely. Rock festivals draw tremendous crowds. Rock festivals attract people from many miles away. Rock festivals feature various popular electronic bands. The various popular electronic bands play for hours on end. The various popular electronic bands play extremely loud music. The extremely loud music doesn't seem to bother the people who attend the rock festivals. The people who attend the rock festivals sometimes listen intently to the rock music and the soloists, but other times the people who attend the rock festivals pay no attention to the rock music or the soloists. The people who attend the rock festivals must enjoy the rock festivals, because the people who attend the rock festivals usually show up at the next rock festival.

Rock Festivals

Rock festivals have been extremely popular during the past several years. *They* often last as long as three days. *They* are advertised widely, *they* draw tremendous crowds, and *they* attract people from many miles away. Rock festivals feature various popular electronic bands. *They* play for hours on end. *They* play extremely loud music. *This* doesn't seem to bother the people who attend *them.* *They* sometimes listen intently to the rock music and the soloists, but other times *they* pay no attention to *them.* People who attend the rock festivals must enjoy *them,* because *they* usually show up at the next *one.*

Assignment 1:A

Copy the following story. Find the pronouns and underline each of them. Then draw an arrow from each pronoun to its antecedent. (The first one has been done for you.)

DAVY CROCKETT I

¹There are many famous Americans. ²Davy Crockett is one of them. ³He was a famous frontiersman. ⁴David Crockett was born in the backwoods of Tennessee in 1786. ⁵He received only four days of formal schooling. ⁶He ran away from home at the age of thirteen. ⁷He didn't return home until several years later.

⁸Davy fell in love when he was eighteen. ⁹The girl he loved wanted him to go back to school. ¹⁰He returned to school for six months, but he didn't enjoy it. ¹¹In spite of his efforts, she didn't marry him after all, but married someone else. ¹²Davy then left school for good. ¹³He never returned to the classroom. ¹⁴His lifetime of experiences educated him well.

Assignment 1:B

Copy the following story. Find the pronouns and underline each of them. Then draw an arrow from each pronoun to its antecedent. (The first one has been done for you.)

DAVY CROCKETT II

¹Davy Crockett later married another girl. ²He and his wife borrowed fifteen dollars. ³They settled down on a farm. ⁴Davy wasn't a very good farmer. ⁵He was much better at hunting bears. ⁶He shot 105 of them in one year. ⁷Davy also loved to tell tales. ⁸The people loved to hear him tell them. ⁹They elected him to the U.S. Congress. ¹⁰He served three terms. ¹¹People in Washington, D.C. could easily recognize him. ¹²He often wore his frontiersman's clothes in that city. ¹³His frontier wisdom also attracted a lot of attention. ¹⁴It was refreshing to them.

Assignment 1:C

Copy the following story. Find the pronouns and underline each of them. Then draw an arrow from each pronoun to its antecedent. (The first one has been done for you.)

DAVY CROCKETT III

¹Davy Crockett fought under Andrew Jackson in 1813. ²Later, Davy went to Texas. ³He fought in the battle of the Alamo. ⁴The Alamo was a mission turned into a fort. ⁵Fewer than two hundred Americans defended it. ⁶More than five thousand Mexican soldiers attacked it. ⁷They stormed the fort with difficulty. ⁸Crockett and the other defenders of the Alamo fought valiantly. ⁹They were all killed in the fight.

¹⁰Davy Crockett has been dead for over a century. ¹¹He still lives on in the memory and hearts of the American people. ¹²He deserves to be remembered by them. ¹³He loved freedom above everything else.

2. PRONOUN AGREEMENT WITH ANTECEDENTS

2.1   A pronoun must agree in number (singular or plural) and gender (masculine, feminine, or neuter) with its antecedent (the word or words that the pronoun represents).

Examples:

    The boy (singular, masculine) is reading. He is reading.
    The boys (plural, masculine) are reading. They are reading.
    The girl (singular, feminine) is reading. She is reading.
    The girls (plural, feminine) are reading. They are reading.
    The book (singular, neuter) is interesting. It is interesting.
    The books (plural, neuter) are interesting. They are interesting.

PRONOUN CHART—PERSONAL PRONOUNS

	SUBJECTIVE		OBJECTIVE		POSSESSIVE MODIFIER		POSSESSIVE PRONOUN		REFLEXIVE	
	Singular	*Plural*	*Singular*	*Plural*	*Singular*	*Plural*	*Singular*	*Plural*	*Singular*	*Plural*
1st Person	I	we	me	us	my	our	mine	ours	myself	ourselves
2nd Person	you	you	you	you	your	your	yours	yours	yourself	yourselves
3rd Person										
masculine	he	they	him	them	his	their	his	theirs	himself	themselves
feminine	she	they	her	them	her	their	hers	theirs	herself	themselves
neuter	it	they	it	them	its	their	its	theirs	itself	themselves

DEMONSTRATIVES
that those
this these

Note: Interrogative pronouns (*who, whom, whose, which, what, where, when, why, how*) are discussed in Chapter 7.
Relative pronouns (*who, whom, whose, which, that*) are discussed in Chapter 11.

2.2 Pronouns representing the same antecedent have **subjective, objective, possessive,** and **reflexive** forms. **Subjective** pronouns are used in subject position.

Example:
   Mary is competent. **She** is also efficient.

Objective pronouns are used in object positions.

Examples:
   The personnel manager hired Mary. Mary's co-workers like **her.** (object of verb)
   The supervisor is happy with **her.** (object of preposition)

Possessive pronouns are used in place of possessives (noun + 's).

Example:
   Mary's work is challenging. **Her** hours are long.

Reflexive pronouns are used:

1. as objects when the subject and the object are the same thing.

Example:
   Mary forces **herself** to get the job done.

2. for emphasis.

Example:
   She **herself** sets the pace.

2.3 In writing, **I** always represents the **writer,** and **you** the **reader.** For this reason it is not usually necessary to use or state the antecedent for these pronouns.

In formal writing, **one** should be used instead of **you** when an impersonal pronoun is desired (the possessive form of **one** is **one's** or **his.**)

Examples:
   You should hand in **your** homework on time.
   One should hand in **his** homework on time. (formal)
   One should hand in **one's** homework on time. (more formal)

Assignment 2:A

Rewrite the following passage. Substitute the correct pronoun for each of the italicized nouns.

TOKYO

[1]Tokyo is the largest city in the world. [2]*Tokyo's* population is over fifteen million. [3]It is predicted that by 1985 *Tokyo's population* will exceed twenty-five million.
   [4]Tokyo is also the capital of Japan. [5]Since 1603, *Tokyo* has been the political, economic, and cultural center of Japan. [6]In that year, Tokugawa Ieyasu [a man] set up *Tokugawa Ieyasu's* shogunate in a castle town. [7]*The castle town* was then called Edo. [8]During the Meiji Restoration in 1868, *Edo's* name was changed to Tokyo.
   [9]Tokyo has been destroyed many times, by fire, earthquake, and bombing. [10]The people of Tokyo have never abandoned *the people of Tokyo's* city. [11]*The people of Tokyo* have rebuilt *Tokyo* every time *Tokyo* has been destroyed. [12]Each time, Tokyo has recovered from destruction to become an even greater city than before.

Assignment 2:B

Rewrite the following passage. Substitute the correct pronoun for each of the italicized nouns.

MOUNT FUJI

[1]Mount Fuji is Japan's most famous mountain. [2]*Mount Fuji* is also Japan's highest mountain. [3]*Mount Fuji* rises 3,776 meters above sea level. [4]Mount Fuji is unique because of *Mount Fuji's* cone shape and the way it rises from the surrounding plain.

[5]There are three mountain climbing paths on Mount Fuji. [6]Buses that travel on the mountain highways carry passengers up to the 1,500 meter level. [7]Many people ride on *the buses that travel on the mountain highways.* [8]Some of the people then try to climb to the top of Mount Fuji. [9]These people are Japanese as well as foreign tourists. [10]All of *these people* do not make it to the top. [11]Climbing Mount Fuji is not easy. [12]*Climbing Mount Fuji* can be very difficult for the unprepared climber.

[13]Many visitors to Mount Fuji do not try to climb *Mount Fuji*. [14]*Many visitors to Mount Fuji* are content to view Mount Fuji from a distance. [15]*Many visitors to Mount Fuji* prefer to spend *many visitors to Mount Fuji's* time seeing the many other beautiful sights of Japan.

Assignment 2:C

Rewrite the following passage. Substitute the correct pronoun for each of the italicized nouns.

HOKKAIDO

[1]Hokkaido is the northernmost island of Japan. [2]*Hokkaido* has not been developed very much because of *Hokkaido's* distance from the main island of Honshu.

[3]Hokkaido's climate is quite cold. [4]*Hokkaido's* average year round temperature is five to seven degrees Centigrade. [5]In January, the temperature may drop to ten degrees Centigrade below zero.

[6]Sapporo is the political, economic, and cultural center of Hokkaido. [7]*Sapporo* was the site of the 1972 Winter Olympics. [8]Athletes from all over the world traveled to Sapporo. [9]*The athletes from all over the world* competed in skiing, ice skating, and other winter sports. [10]Tourists from all over the world came to watch *the athletes from all over the world* compete.

[11]Hokkaido's annual attraction is the Snow Festival. [12]*The Snow Festival* is held in Sapporo every February. [13]Sapporo's central plaza is filled with gigantic sculptures of historical, modern, and imaginary characters made of snow. [14]*The gigantic sculptures of historical, modern, and imaginary characters made of snow* are very impressive. [15]*The gigantic sculptures of historical, modern, and imaginary characters made of snow* may be over twenty feet high. [16]*The gigantic sculptures of historical, modern, and imaginary characters* look like dragons, samurai warriors, or even famous Japanese temples. [17]Visitors from far away travel to Sapporo to look at *the gigantic sculptures of historical, modern, and imaginary characters made of snow.*

3. CLARITY OF PRONOUN ANTECEDENTS

The antecedent of a pronoun must be clear to the reader.

In a paragraph, the noun (antecedent) is usually stated near the beginning. Pronouns may then be substituted for the same noun used later, unless (1) other possible antecedents have the same number (singular or plural) and gender (masculine, feminine, or neuter), and/or (2) the pronoun is used excessively.

If the use of a pronoun may be confusing to the reader, use the full noun or noun phrase instead of the pronoun.

Example of confusing pronoun use:

Trees are useful to man. The leaves give off oxygen. The trunks and branches provide wood. I feel sad when they fall to the ground.

Which of these drawings is described in the paragraph above?

The above paragraph is confusing because the pronoun *they* could refer to *leaves, trees,* or *branches*.

The occasional use of the antecedent noun improves the composition, particularly when the topic emphasis changes. Compare the use of pronouns in these two paragraphs.

Coconut Trees

Coconut trees grow in tropical and semi-tropical climates. ***They*** grow almost anywhere. ***They*** grow on the seashore, and ***they*** grow at higher elevations. ***They*** are very useful, as they provide most of man's necessities. ***They*** provide food for people, and ***they*** furnish fuel for fires. ***They*** provide oil for soap and other products. ***They*** supply material for building houses. ***They*** furnish shade either as trees or when woven as blinds, and ***they*** are used for mats and clothing.

Coconut Trees

Coconut trees grow in tropical and semi-tropical climates. ***They*** grow almost anywhere. ***They*** grow on the seashore, and they grow at higher elevations. **Coconut trees** are very useful, as ***they*** provide most of man's necessities. ***They*** provide food for people and ***they*** furnish fuel for fires. ***They*** provide oil for soap and other products. ***They*** supply material for building houses. **Coconut trees** furnish shade either as trees or when woven as blinds, and ***they*** are used for mats and clothing.

Assignment 3:A

Rewrite the following passage, substituting pronouns for nouns where appropriate. You must decide which nouns should be replaced by pronouns and which pronouns should be used to replace them. Make sure that each pronoun you use clearly refers to its antecedent and agrees with it.

OCEANS

[1]The earth is a water world. [2]Oceans dominate the earth. [3]Oceans cover over two-thirds of the earth. [4]Oceans regulate the weather. [5]So far, man has utilized only the available arable land. [6]Man is rapidly exhausting the available arable land's resources. [7]The ocean may be the answer to man's needs. [8]Up until now, the ocean has been used only as a highway for ships and as a hunting ground for fishermen. [9]The ocean may provide man with food and minerals. [10]The ocean has more plants and animals than the land. [11]Ocean currents have been charted, but man must know much more about the ocean if man is to use the ocean for man's advantage. [12]Can man use the ocean for a dumping ground for man's radioactive waste and then expect to eat the ocean's produce? [13]If man contaminates the ocean, can man still expect the ocean to retain the ocean's productivity?

Assignment 3:B

Rewrite the following passage, substituting pronouns for nouns where appropriate. You must decide which nouns should be replaced by pronouns and which pronouns should be used to replace them. Make sure that each pronoun you use clearly refers to its antecedent and agrees with it.

TYPEWRITERS

[1] Until 1867 people had to write in longhand. [2] Although people could use feather quills, steel pen points, fountain pens, and pencils, people still had to write in longhand.

[3] Typewriters are mechanical instruments which make an impression on paper when keys are struck. [4] Typewriters are used in homes, schools, offices, etc. [5] Almost all secretaries use typewriters daily.

[6] The typewriter was invented in 1867 by a United States journalist. [7] The typewriter was patented by a United States journalist in 1868.

[8] Manual typewriters were used for many years. [9] Manual typewriters can be used anywhere. [10] Manual typewriters do not use electricity. [11] The highest recorded speeds for typing on a manual typewriter are listed in the *Guiness Book of World Records*. [12] The highest speeds for typing on a manual typewriter are 170 words per minute for one minute and an average of 147 words per minute for one hour of steady typing.

[13] Electric typewriters are now used in many places. [14] Electric typewriters are easier to use and typists can attain higher speeds on electric typewriters. [15] The official record on an electric typewriter is 216 words per minute. [16] For one hour, the official record on an electric typewriter is 149 words per minute.

Assignment 3:C

Rewrite the following passage, substituting pronouns for nouns where appropriate. You must decide which nouns should be replaced by pronouns and which pronouns should be used to replace them. Make sure each pronoun you use clearly refers to its antecedent and agrees with it.

CONSTANTINE

[1] The first Christian ruler of the Roman Empire was Constantine I. [2] The first Christian ruler of the Roman Empire was also known as Constantine the Great. [3] The first Christian ruler of the Roman Empire's full name was Flavius Valerius Aurelius Constantinus. [4] The first Christian ruler of the Roman Empire was born about A.D. 280.

[5] Constantine fought as a soldier in Egypt and Persia. [6] Constantine's father was also a soldier and one of the rulers of the Roman Empire. [7] Constantine and Constantine's father fought together in Britain.

[8] Constantine became a Christian in an unusual way. [9] In the year 312 A.D. Constantine marched on Rome with Constantine's armies to attack Maxentius, his rival. [10] The night before the battle, Constantine had a vision. [11] The vision convinced Constantine to become a Christian. [12] Constantine saw a flaming cross in the sky. [13] Beneath the flaming cross in the sky the words "By this sign thou shalt conquer" were written. [14] Constantine adopted the cross as a symbol. [15] Constantine had the cross put on the sails of Constantine's ships. [16] Constantine's men put the cross on Constantine's men's shields and flags. [17] The next day, Constantine defeated Maxentius.

[18] After defeating all of Constantine's other rivals, Constantine became the only ruler of the entire Roman world. [19] Sunday became the day of worship. [20] Later, Constantine ordered a meeting held at Nicaea. [21] The meeting's purpose was to settle disputes over Christ's divinity.

[22] In the year 330, Constantine established a new capital in the East. [23] The new capital in the East was named Constantinople—"The City of Constantine." [24] Today, "The City of Constantine" is called Istanbul.

4. DUMMY SUBJECTS

4.1 A dummy subject is used because in written English every sentence must have a subject. When *it* is used as a dummy subject, it does not have an antecedent.

Examples:
   It rains a lot here.
   It's a warm day.

In some cases the true subject has been shifted toward the end of the sentence. (This process is explained in Chapter 13.) The dummy *it* takes the original subject's place.

Examples:
>It is hard to believe what you say.
>It's a miracle that he survived.

4.2 *There* is also a dummy subject. However, aux-word or verb agreement depends on the noun or noun phrase which follows the verb or aux-word rather than on the dummy subject *there*.

Examples:
>There is an apple in the basket. (singular count noun)
>There are several apples in the basket. (plural count noun)
>There is excitement in the air. (noncount noun)
>There seems to be some trouble here. (noun phrase)

Note that *there*, like the dummy subject *it*, has no meaning. It only functions as a dummy subject, permitting a noun or noun phrase to follow.

There is also an adverb of place which designates a certain location already mentioned or a location not near the speaker.

Assignment 4:A

In the following paragraph, each it *has been italicized and numbered. On your paper, after each number, write a* P *if the* it *is a pronoun and a* D *if the* it *is a dummy subject.*

A COLD DAY

It's now the middle of winter and *it*'s a very cold day. The temperature outside is fifteen degrees Fahrenheit, and
1   2

it is dropping steadily. *It* has been a long time since anyone has felt comfortable outside. Inside the house *it* is
3   4   5

warm and cozy. I have a fire and *it* keeps me warm. *It* is pleasant to watch the flame flicker as *it* throws shadows
                                  6   7   8

on the walls. However, *it* is necessary for me to go outside and bring in some more wood if I expect to keep *it*
                       9   10

burning during the night. *It* is a task I dread, but the sooner I do *it* the sooner I can return to my pleasant room
                          11   12

and *it*s cozy comfort. I had better get at *it*.
    13   14

Assignment 4:B

In the following paragraph, each it *has been italicized and numbered. On your paper, after each number, write a* P *if the* it *is a pronoun and a* D *if the* it *is a dummy subject.*

A GARDEN

It is spring. Suddenly, *it*'s time to get out-of-doors and get to work. *It* rains a lot during the spring, so *it*'s necessary
1   2   3   4

to work when one can. *It* is necessary to trim the deadwood from the trees and shrubs. *It*'s important to oil the
                      5   6

lawnmower as *it* may have rusted a bit during the winter. The garden must be planted. *It* should have vegetables as
             7   8

well as flowers.

SENTENCE CONSTRUCTION

When summer comes, *it* would be nice to go fishing, but the garden needs a lot of care. *It* needs to be
                                   9   10
cultivated. *It* also needs to be watered and weeded. *It* seems that the work never ends.
          11   12

It pays dividends, however, to raise a garden. In addition to the satisfaction of seeing things grow, *it*
13   14
produces food for the body and flowers for the soul.

Assignment 4:C

In the following paragraph, each it *has been italicized and numbered. On your paper, after each number, write a* P *if the* it *is a pronoun and a* D *if the* it *is a dummy subject.*

DAYDREAMS

Most of us, like Walter Mitty*, have performed a heroic deed or two. *It* might have been one of courage, *it* might
                                                                                    1   2
have been one of strength, or *it* might have been one of nobility. *It* is amazing what one can accomplish when he
                             3   4
daydreams. *It* seems like nothing is impossible. *It* may be dangerous to daydream, since *it* is a jolt when the
              5   6   7
dream is over and reality calls one back to the real world. *It* may be very hard to achieve the dream, so one might
                                                                                                 8
not even attempt *it* even though *it* is possible. On the other hand, when the dream is impossible to achieve in
                     9   10
reality, *it* is better not to attempt to achieve *it*. *It* is fun to dream, though, isn't *it*?
        11   12 13   14

*James Thurber, "The Secret Life of Walter Mitty," *My World and Welcome to It* (New York: Harcourt Brace Jovanovich, 1937).

Assignment 4.1:A

In the following paragraph, each there *has been italicized and numbered. On your paper, after each number, write a* D *if the* there *is a dummy subject and a* P *if the* there *is a place.*

FAIRY TALES

There are many fairy tales in story books. Found *there* are "Jack and the Beanstalk" and "Cinderella." *There*
  1   2   3
is also an old favorite of mine—"Rumpelstiltskin." "Beauty and the Beast" is *there* too. *There* seems to be a
                                                                                                  4   5
strange fascination in these often-told tales for young and old. In my mind's eye I can still see the books *there* on
                                                                                                                                                              6
the shelf in my old room. *There* is my mother, too, and the rocking chair she sat in as she read these stories to me.
                              7
There were books of nursery rhymes *there* too, along with the fairy tales. *There* were "Little Boy Blue,"
  8   9   10
"Goosey, Goosey Gander," and "Little Jack Horner" within those pages. Today *there* are cartoons and TV
                                                                                                    11
programs to take the place of the fairy tales. *There* seems to be too much competition for the princes and
                                                   12
princesses, the ogres and the witches that are found *there* in the old silent books.
                                                         13

Assignment 4.1:B

In the following paragraph, each there *has been italicized and numbered. On your paper, after each number, write a* D *if the* there *is a dummy subject and a* P *if the* there *is a place.*

THE CIRCUS

Everyone who is young in heart loves a circus. *There*₁ are acts involving clowns, trapeze artists, high wire performers, and trained animals. Wild animals are *there*₂ as well. *There*₃ are also side shows to view the fat man, the bearded lady, and other sights, so be sure to take some extra money when you go *there*₄.

*There*₅ may also be guessing games and games of chance in addition to a huge ferris wheel and other enticing rides. It's fun for the family to go *there*₆, as *there*₇ is sure to be something for everybody—young and old. *There*₈ are so many things to see and hear at a three-ring circus that it is impossible to take in everything. Hopefully, they'll all be *there*₉ again when the circus rolls around next time, so save your money and we'll plan on going again next year.

Assignment 4.1:C

In the following paragraph, each there *has been italicized and numbered. On your paper, after each number, write a* D *if the* there *is a dummy subject and a* P *if the* there *is a place.*

THE ICEMAN

In grandmother's day *there*₁ were many occupations which do not exist today. For example, *there*₂ was the iceman. He had a large truck with a big insulated box on the back. Huge blocks of ice were kept *there*₃. He delivered sections of these to houses along his route. He would look at the windows and, if cards were displayed *there*₄, he would chip off the amount of ice indicated on the card. Then, the iceman would seize the piece with his tongs, sling it over his leather-clad shoulder, carry it into the house, and once *there*₅ place it in the ice box. The woman of the house often had to mop up the watery trail left by the melting ice. *There*₆ were always lots of children in the street around the van waiting to catch any small chips of ice that might fall *there*₇. Occasionally, *there*₈ was a friendly iceman who would chip off a few small fragments and toss them into the crowd of children who vied with one another to be the lucky recipient of a cold chunk of ice. Automatic refrigeration has brought an end to the coming of the iceman, but *there*₉ are many who still recall those good old days with nostalgia.

4
AUX-WORDS

1. FORMS OF AUX-WORDS

An important kind of function word is the auxiliary. These words are often called helping or auxiliary verbs and/or modals. In this book we call them aux-words.

Following are the forms of some of the common English aux-words:

Present	Past
is, am, are (forms of *be*)	was, were (forms of *be*)
have, has	had
do, does	did
can, will, may, shall, must	could, would, might, should
	(*must* does not have a past form)

Should (for obligation) is used in both the present and the past. *Had to* is the counterpart of *must* in the past.

The aux-words *can, could, will, would, may, might, shall, should,* and *must* belong to a special group called **modals**.

Contractions combining aux-words with *not* are also considered aux-words.

Present	Past
isn't, aren't	wasn't, weren't
haven't, hasn't	hadn't
don't, doesn't	didn't
can't, won't (mayn't and shan't are seldom used)	couldn't, wouldn't
mustn't	

Although aux-words have only present and past forms (or tenses) they may be used to show many different times (this is explained in Chapter 6).

Assignment 1:A

Find the aux-words in the passage below. On your paper write the number of each sentence and the aux-words you find in that sentence.

BLACKBOARDS

[1]Blackboards are very useful things. [2]Educators, businessmen, or scientists can use them in their work. [3]Many people don't appreciate the advantages of blackboards. [4]A well-used blackboard can be an invaluable aid to communication.

⁵A blackboard doesn't cost a lot of money. ⁶It doesn't require electricity or gasoline. ⁷It can be used over and over. ⁸A person can write on it. ⁹The writing may be easily erased. ¹⁰Something else can then be written in the same place.

¹¹Blackboard use is not without its hazards. ¹²Misusing a blackboard will result in problems. ¹³An uncared-for blackboard will deteriorate. ¹⁴The surface will crack. ¹⁵It may get too smooth to use.

¹⁶A teacher may purposely misuse a blackboard to wake up sleeping students. ¹⁷Scratching fingernails on a blackboard will make a terrible noise. ¹⁸Holding a piece of chalk the wrong way will also result in an awful sound. ¹⁹Ignorance may cause people to mistreat a blackboard. ²⁰Everyone should learn to use a blackboard properly.

Assignment 1:B

Find the aux-words in the passage below. On your paper write the number of each sentence and the aux-words you find in that sentence.

CRABS

¹Crabs are strange animals. ²These shellfish can live in or out of water. ³Their five pairs of walking legs are long and spindly but strong. ⁴Their muscles are inside their skeleton. ⁵A crab's eyes are found on movable stalks. ⁶They can be extended or retracted. ⁷Crabs don't walk forward. ⁸Crabs don't walk backward. ⁹They can only walk sideways.

¹⁰There are many different kinds of crabs. ¹¹Hermit crabs must live in shells discarded by other sea creatures. ¹²When they outgrow one shell, they must find another, larger one. ¹³The tiny pea crab can be found living inside the shell of an oyster. ¹⁴The giant king crab may measure ten feet from tip to tip of its claws. ¹⁵In spring, tropical land crabs may be seen migrating by the thousands to the sea to lay their eggs. ¹⁶Nothing will stop them or make them change course. ¹⁷The fiddler crab is the type most commonly seen on the beach. ¹⁸Some types of crabs are valued as food. ¹⁹Others are not good to eat. ²⁰All crabs are fascinating to observe.

Assignment 1:C

Find the aux-words in the passage below. On your paper write the number of each sentence and the aux-words you find in that sentence.

LEARNING A NEW LANGUAGE

¹Learning a new language is usually hard work. ²Students must spend many hours speaking, reading, and writing the new language. ³They are required to do many exercises which may be uninteresting or even boring. ⁴They may also have to spend many hours in a language lab where they must concentrate on the sounds of the new tongue so they will recognize these sounds and also so they can produce them. ⁵The sounds and grammar of a new language are often quite different from those of the student's native tongue and thus may be confusing to the learner. ⁶Many times students feel they have mastered the new language, only to find that they can not communicate with native speakers. ⁷Many will give up their study while others will renew their efforts to master the new tongue.

2. SUBJECT/AUX-WORD AGREEMENT (PRESENT TENSE)

In the present tense some aux-words have more than one form. The form used depends on the subject of the sentence it is used in.

Am is used only when the subject is the pronoun *I*.

Is is used with singular and noncount subjects (except the pronoun *you*).

Are is used with plural subjects (and the pronoun *you*).

Has is used with singular and noncount subjects (except the pronouns *I* and *you*).

Have is used with plural subjects (and the pronouns *I* and *you*).

Does is used with singular subjects (except the pronouns *I* and *you*).

Do is used with plural subjects (and the pronouns *I* and *you*).

Other aux-words (the modals) have only one present tense form.

can, may, will, shall, must

Examples:
I *am* studying English.
My brother *is* studying English.
My friends *are* studying English.
You *are* studying English.

He *has* studied English for a long time.
I *have* studied English for a long time.
You *have* studied English for a long time.

My brother *does* not write very well.
I *do* not write very well.
You *do* not write very well.

I *can* come.
My brother *can* come.
All family members *can* come.

I *may* go.
Others *may* go.

My dad *will* try to learn English.
My parents *will* try to learn English.

My brother *must* go tomorrow.
All the students *must* go tomorrow.

Assignment 2:A

Rewrite the following passage. Write is *or* are, *whichever is correct, in place of the blanks.*

CROCODILIANS I

[1]The crocodile and alligator _____ reptiles, a major class of animals that also includes snakes, lizards, and turtles. [2]There _____ about twenty-five species of reptiles belonging to a group called crocodilians. [3]Crocodiles, alligators, caymans, and gavials _____ all crocodilians.

[4]A crocodilian _____ not very pretty. [5]Its skin _____ made up of many small bony plates and scales. [6]Its long jaws, sharp teeth, and ugly appearance _____ terrifying to many people.

[7]All crocodilians _____ similar, but there _____ ways of telling one type of crocodilian from another. [8]The snout of the true crocodile _____ long and tapering. [9]The head _____ almost triangular. [10]The snout of the alligator _____ broad and rounded.

[11]The cayman's snout _____ also broad and rounded, but the snout of a gavial _____ extremely long and thin.

¹²All kinds of noises _____ made by crocodilians. ¹³Booming, barking, croaking, and grunting _____ only a few of them.

Assignment 2:B

Rewrite the following passage. Write is *or* are, *whichever is correct, in place of the blanks.*

CROCODILIANS II

¹All crocodilians _____ good swimmers. ²Most of them spend their lives in or near lakes, rivers, or swamps. ³Their long powerful tails _____ used to propel them through the water. ⁴Their short legs _____ held close to the body.

⁵A crocodilian _____ well equipped for floating at the water's surface. ⁶Its eyes, ears, and nostrils _____ on the top of its head and snout. ⁷They remain above the waterline while the rest of the crocodilian's body _____ floating beneath the surface.

⁸A crocodilian _____ also capable of diving beneath the surface. ⁹It _____ reported that some crocodilians _____ capable of staying under water for as long as five hours at a time.

¹⁰Crocodilians _____ good hunters. ¹¹Sometimes a crocodilian floats just beneath the surface waiting to snap up a duck, muskrat, or other water animal which _____ swimming by. ¹²The crocodilian also waits near a watering hole to seize an animal that comes to drink. ¹³Animals as large as deer and cattle _____ fair game for a large crocodilian. ¹⁴It grips them with its strong jaws and drags them into the water. ¹⁵Once the prey _____ in the water, the crocodilian drags it beneath the surface to drown. ¹⁶Even people _____ sometimes attacked by large crocodilians. ¹⁷All crocodilians _____ dangerous when cornered or wounded.

Assignment 2:C

Rewrite the following passage. Write is *or* are, *whichever is correct, in place of the blanks.*

CROCODILIANS III

¹The nests of some crocodilians _____ made of plant materials. ²Others _____ simply holes scooped in a riverbank. ³From twenty to ninety crocodilian eggs _____ laid at a time. ⁴The eggs _____ long and white with a hard, thick shell.

⁵Crocodilians _____ tiny when they _____ born, but some of them _____ very large when they _____ grown. ⁶An adult American alligator weighs about 500 pounds. ⁷One American crocodile _____ reported to have weighed 1,350 pounds!

⁸Newborn crocodilians _____ easy prey for other animals. ⁹A recently hatched crocodilian _____ almost defenseless. ¹⁰Many young crocodilians _____ eaten by larger animals.

¹¹Once it reaches adulthood, however, a large crocodilian _____ relatively safe. ¹²It _____ possible for it to live a long time. ¹³The oldest alligators on record _____ more than fifty years old.

¹⁴If there _____ a long period of hot, dry weather, the crocodilian buries itself deep in the mud. ¹⁵There the animal goes into a deep summer sleep which _____ called estivation. ¹⁶If the weather _____ too cold, crocodilians go into a deep winter sleep called hibernation. ¹⁷They wake up when conditions _____ better.

Assignment 2.1:A

Rewrite the following passage. Write have *or* has, *whichever is correct, in place of the blanks.*

A DISCOURAGING DAY

¹_____ life ever disappointed you unexpectedly? ²_____ a day ever discouraged you completely? ³If so, you can sympathize with me. ⁴Today _____ been a very discouraging day for me. ⁵I _____ had a very difficult time. ⁶I _____ tried to do many things, but not a single one _____ succeeded. ⁷I made great plans at the beginning of the day, but now, as I look back, all my plans _____ failed. ⁸So many things _____ backfired today that I don't even dare try anything else. ⁹I feel like going back to bed. ¹⁰Everything _____ gone wrong and I _____ lost hope that anything will turn out right. ¹¹It seems like everything _____ been a disappointment. ¹²I _____ had difficult days before, but there _____ never been one like today. ¹³I hope you _____ never had a day like this.

Aux-words 37

Assignment 2.1:B

Rewrite the following passage. Write have *or* has, *whichever is correct, in place of the blanks.*

SUCCESS IN LIFE

¹I _____ always dreamed of being a great success. ²Although I _____ attempted many things, I still _____ not found anything that I _____ been successful at or that _____ appealed to me.

³Other members of my family _____ all been successful. ⁴My father _____ become a captain in the Air Force. ⁵My mother _____ been elected to Congress. ⁶Although it _____ taken him seven years, one of my brothers _____ just graduated from college. ⁷My sister _____ earned her degree in medicine. ⁸My other brother is not the academic type, but he _____ been very successful as an explorer. ⁹He _____ just discovered a new tributary to the Amazon River which _____ been named after him.

¹⁰I'm the only one in the family who _____ not achieved something worthwhile. ¹¹My folks _____ all given up on me, but I _____ not. ¹²Someday, I will find what I _____ always been looking for, and I will be successful too.

Assignment 2.1:C

Rewrite the following passage. Write have *or* has, *whichever is correct, in place of the blanks.*

A BOOK OF WORLD RECORDS

¹For the past several years, a book of world records _____ been published. ²So many people _____ bought it that it _____ become a best seller. ³Writing the book _____ not been easy for the authors. ⁴They _____ been careful to include only authenticated records, although authenticating the records _____ at times been difficult. ⁵Many people _____ tried to get their names in the book, but only a few _____ succeeded.

⁶If you _____ ever read the book, you will know that it contains some very unusual records. ⁷One man whose name appears in the book _____ surmounted the problems of playing a violin under water and gives concerts from a swimming pool. ⁸The English language _____ made it into the book by having the largest vocabulary—490,000 words plus another 300,000 technical terms. ⁹One

38   SENTENCE CONSTRUCTION

man _____ walked from Vienna to Paris—a distance of 871 miles—on his hands! [10]Another _____ pulled a locomotive and a truck weighing 135.5 tons with his teeth! [11]An Australian man took a shower that lasted 202 hours, and an English woman rocked in a rocking chair for 432 hours. [12]An English man _____ attended 4,160 theatrical productions in 20 years of theatre going and is still going. [13]There _____ never been a record-breaker like Jesse Owens, who broke six world records on a single day in 1935. [14]So many people _____ bought the record book that the book itself _____ claimed an enviable record as the fastest selling book in the world.

3. SUBJECT/AUX-WORD AGREEMENT (PAST TENSE)

3.1   There are two past tense forms of *be*: *was* and *were*.

Was is used with singular subjects except the singular pronoun *you*.

Were is used with plural subjects and the singular pronoun *you*.

Examples:

Present	Past
I *am* studying English.	I *was* studying English.
My sister *is* studying English.	My sister *was* studying English.
My friends *are* studying English.	My friends *were* studying English.
You *are* studying English.	You *were* studying English.

3.2   Except for the forms of *be* (*is, am, are*), all aux-words which have more than one form in the present tense have only one past tense form.

Present	Past
have, has	had
do, does	did
can	could
will	would
may	might
shall	should
must	(*must* has no past form. *Had to* is used in the past tense.)

Examples:

Present	Past
Joe *has* done his homework.	Joe *had* done his homework.
The other students *have* done their homework.	The other students *had* done their homework.
I *don't* know the answer.	I *didn't* know the answer.
My friend *doesn't* know the answer.	My friend *didn't* know the answer.

Assignment 3:A

Rewrite the following paragraph substituting In 1895 *for* Now. *You will have to change the aux-words to agree with this new time.*

PASSENGER PIGEONS

[1]Now we are crossing the great plains of North America. [2]Thousands of birds are seen daily. [3]The greatest flocks are the Passenger Pigeons, numbering in the thousands. [4]They are different from the birds back home as their tails are longer than their wings. [5]These birds don't fly high beyond our reach. [6]Instead, the huge flocks are right above our heads. [7]Everyone is very excited about shooting them because one doesn't have to be a good marksman to hit these targets. [8]Anyone can shoot down a bird or two with every shot. [9]Sometimes we will kill hundreds in a day. [10]I don't think we will ever see the end of the Passenger Pigeon.

Assignment 3:B

Rewrite the following paragraphs substituting Many years ago *for* Today. *You will have to change the aux-words to agree with this new time.*

THE SAMOAN MATAI*

[1]Today in Samoa matais are very powerful. [2]They are able to decide for the entire family or village. [3]They do not have to consult others in making decisions. [4]They can assign anyone to do certain tasks. [5]They can collect wages.

[6]However, being a matai is also a responsibility. [7]A matai is expected to provide for his family or village. [8]He is responsible for the welfare of everyone under his leadership.

[9]Matais may be elected by the family. [10]The top village matai is usually elected by the family matais. [11]Once elected, a matai is usually a matai for life.

*Matai = Chief

Assignment 3:C

Rewrite the following paragraph substituting One of the older materials *for* One of today's materials. *You will have to change the aux-words to agree with this new time.*

TAPA CLOTH

[1]One of today's materials is tapa cloth which is a fabric made from trees. [2]It is used for clothing and bedding by many people on South Pacific islands. [3]Thin strips of bark from the paper mulberry tree are pounded into 18-inch wide strips. [4]These strips are glued together with a paste made from the tapioca root. [5]The material can then be painted with dyes which are made from other plants. [6]The resulting material can be fashioned into clothes or bedding. [7]It is warm and quite durable. [8]One drawback of tapa cloth, however, is that it can not be washed with water. [9]It can only be put in the sun or aired to cleanse it.

4. YES/NO QUESTIONS AND AUX-WORDS

4.1 Aux-words are used to form:

1. yes/no questions (questions that are answered *yes* or *no*),
2. negative statements or questions, and
3. emphatic statements.

Aux-words are also used with tag and *wh*-questions (this is explained in Chapter 7) and as pro-verbs (this is explained in Chapter 10).

4.2 Yes/No questions are questions that can be answered with *yes* or *no*.

To change a simple statement into a written yes/no question,

1. find the aux-word—a part of the predicate which follows the subject and precedes the remainder of the predicate, and
2. move the aux-word to the front of the sentence.

Examples:

Don Quixote was a dreamer.   (aux-word = *was*)
Was Don Quixote   a dreamer?

He couldn't really change the world.   (aux-word = *couldn't*)
Couldn't he   really change the world?

4.3 The process of moving the aux-word to change a statement into a yes/no question indicates the complete subject of the sentence. The word/words between the first (statement) aux-word position and the second (question) aux-word position are the subject.

Examples:

Christmas is coming soon.
Is Christmas   coming soon?   (subject = Christmas)

The brown packages lying on the table are ready to be mailed.
Are the brown packages lying on the table   ready to be mailed?
        (subject = the brown packages lying on the table)

The decorations, tinsel, and bright lights for the tree have been unpacked.
Have the decorations, tinsel, and bright lights for the tree   been unpacked?
        (subject = the decorations, tinsel, and bright lights for the tree)

Assignment 4:A

Rewrite each of the following affirmative sentences into a yes/no *question by moving the aux-word from its position after the subject to a position in front of the subject.*

SHARKS I

1. A shark's primary food is fish, sea turtles, birds, and other sharks.

2. They will feed on almost anything found in the sea.

3. Most sharks are dangerous to man.

4. They will attack without warning.

5. The great white shark is the most famous man-eater.

6. It is always hungry and never afraid.

7. Its razor-sharp, triangular teeth can slice through anything.

8. Sharks can grow new ones when they lose their teeth attacking boats.

9. Most fishermen do not catch sharks for food.

10. The refuse from cleaning their fish is dumped into the sea.

11. This is food for the sharks.

12. The number of sharks has increased in the past twenty or thirty years.

Assignment 4:B
Rewrite each of the following affirmative sentences into a yes/no question by moving the aux-word from its position after the subject to a position in front of the subject.

SHARKS II

1. The tiger shark is the most common of the sharks.

2. It is normally a slow swimmer.

3. It is very fast when chasing something.

4. Tiger sharks have frequently been seen in shallow water.

5. They have often attacked men.

6. They do not seem to need a reason.

7. Many strange things have been found in sharks' stomachs.

8. They will eat anything.

9. A roll of roofing paper was once found in a tiger shark's stomach.

10. There was also a keg of nails.

11. Sharks can be of use to man.

12. Fine leather can be made from tiger shark skin.

13. The oil from the liver is also valuable.

Assignment 4:C

Rewrite each of the following affirmative sentences into a yes/no question by moving the aux-word from its position after the subject to a position in front of the subject.

SHARKS III

1. Men have been seeking a shark repellent for a long time.

2. Many things have been tried.

3. These have included mechanical, electrical, and chemical devices.

4. A thing successful on one shark does not seem to work on another.

5. Shark nets are used to keep sharks away from bathing beaches in Australia and South Africa.

6. The sharks are caught in the net by their gills as they swim toward the shore.

7. Shark fisheries have reduced the number of sharks in some areas.

8. The most effective control of sharks would be to catch them.

9. Sharks could be used for food.

10. They could also be used for fertilizer, oil, leather, and many other things.

11. Sharks would then be benefactors of man instead of his enemies.

5. HIDDEN AUX-WORDS

Some statements have no apparent aux-word. The aux-word is hidden. It is contained within the time-included verb form. (Time-included and timeless verb forms are explained in Chapter 5.)

The hidden aux-words are:
> *do*
> *does*
> *did*

To form a yes/no question from these statements, the hidden aux-word (*do*, *does*, or *did*) must be taken out and moved to the front of the sentence. The time-included verb form then changes to the timeless base form.

Examples:

      The student goes to school every day.   The student studied English last year.
Does the student go to school every day?   **Did** the student study English last year?

      The students go to school every day.   The students studied English last year.
Do the students go to school every day?   **Did** the students study English last year?

SENTENCE CONSTRUCTION

Assignment 5:A

Rewrite each of the following affirmative sentences into a question by moving the aux-word to a position in front of the subject. You will have to supply the hidden aux-words.

HOLIDAYS

1. Everyone enjoys a holiday.

2. Holidays commemorate religious or political events, and national or international occasions.

3. Many cultures share holidays.

4. Others relate to only one culture.

5. People use different calendars.

6. They even celebrate the New Year at different times.

7. Christmas, a holiday of the Christian world, occurs on one day, December 25th.

8. Hanukkah, a Jewish holiday, lasts for several days.

9. Many countries have some sort of harvest holiday.

10. The United States has Thanksgiving.

11. Ancient Hawaiians observed the Makahiki.

12. Independence initiated many in-country holidays.

13. The United States celebrates the Fourth of July.

14. Fiji commemorates October 10th.

15. Korea's independence day occurs on August 15th.

Assignment 5:B
Rewrite each of the following affirmative sentences into a question by moving the aux-word to a position in front of the subject. You will have to supply the hidden aux-words.

POLLUTION

1. Many people suffer from respiratory diseases.

2. Smog, caused by pollutants, contributes to their discomfort.

3. Air pollution aggravates their condition.

4. Government agencies monitor pollution levels.

5. Some cities broadcast smog alerts.

6. This warns people to stay indoors and limit their physical activity.

7. Federal and state government laws prohibit excess pollution.

8. Automobile exhausts contaminate the air.

9. Automobile emissions standards help control this problem.

SENTENCE CONSTRUCTION

10. Heavy industry pollutes the environment.

11. The elimination of pollutants from this source increases production costs.

12. The health advantages of a clean environment outweigh these economic disadvantages.

Assignment 5:C

Rewrite each of the following affirmative sentences into a question by moving the aux-word to a position in front of the subject. You will have to supply the hidden aux-words.

EARLY AGRICULTURE

1. People of earlier times wandered from place to place to find food.

2. Some decided to plant grain seeds.

3. They stayed in one place.

4. They raised only a few kinds of crops.

5. Explorers sailed off to new lands.

6. They found many different kinds of food.

7. They took seeds and roots home with them.

8. The people planted these.

9. This enlarged their diet.

10. The people had a variety of fruit and melons in addition to the grains.

11. This made them happy with their permanent establishments.

Assignment 5.1:A

Rewrite each of the following affirmative sentences into a yes/no question by moving the aux-word to a position in front of the subject. In some sentences you will have to supply the hidden aux-words.

MARY'S ENGLISH

1. Mary is a college student this semester.

2. She speaks a little English.

3. She has trouble writing it.

4. She is interested in improving her English skills.

5. She has enrolled in an intensive English program.

6. She doesn't take any other classes.

7. Mary plans on enrolling in other classes later.

8. There are many other students like Mary in the English program.

9. They work hard to learn to write English.

10. They may also take typing classes.

48   SENTENCE CONSTRUCTION

11. They will eventually master English.

12. They can then take classes in their major fields.

Assignment 5.1:B

Rewrite each of the following affirmative sentences into a yes/no question by moving the aux-word to a position in front of the subject. In some sentences you will have to supply the hidden aux-words.

THE HOLIDAY SEASON

1. Christmas is always fun.

2. We spend Christmas Eve singing Christmas carols.

3. Favorite stories are repeated year after year.

4. Family members don't have to work or go to school.

5. Christmas dinner is a festive meal.

6. There is always lots of special food.

7. We spend the holiday season visiting friends and relatives.

8. New Year's Day comes one week later.

9. Everyone celebrates New Year's Eve.

10. There are many parties.

11. There is lots of good food and drink.

12. People make resolutions which are never kept.

13. The holiday season seems to be over too soon.

14. We are always sad to see these holidays end.

Assignment 5.1:C

Rewrite each of the following affirmative sentences into a yes/no question by moving the aux-word to a position in front of the subject. In some sentences you will have to supply the hidden aux-words.

THIS CLASS

1. The students in this class come from many different backgrounds.

2. Some of them grew up in this area.

3. Others have recently moved here from far away.

4. They all need to improve their writing skills.

5. Most of them try hard in class.

6. They complete all their assignments conscientiously.

7. They think about what they are doing.

8. A few of them don't understand the true purpose of the class.

9. These students fail to realize that the class is designed to help them.

10. They continually fight against it.

11. One tries to think of ways to get out of doing the homework.

12. Another cheats on the tests.

13. These students don't realize that they are only cheating themselves.

14. The real test is whether or not their writing truly improves to an acceptable level.

15. Writing correctly in many different situations and at various different times will be the true exam.

16. This test will face them many times in life long after this class is finished.

6. NEGATIVES AND AUX-WORDS

All negative sentences using *not* require an aux-word. The aux-word may precede the *not* or combine with it in a contraction.

When a statement contains only a hidden aux-word, that aux-word (*do, does,* or *did*) must appear before the *not*.

Example:
    John works hard.
    John does not work hard.

When making a yes/no question from a negative statement with an aux-word and *not,* only the aux-word moves to the new position in front of the subject.

Example:
    John will not fail this class.
    Will John   not fail this class?

However, when the aux-word is contracted with the *not,* the entire unit is moved to the new position in front of the subject.

Example:
    John won't fail this class.
    Won't John   fail this class?

Both of these examples have the same meaning. However, the contracted form is less formal. (Writing is usually more formal than speech.)

Assignment 6:A

Rewrite the following affirmative sentences as negative sentences. You will have to supply the hidden aux-word. Your new title will be "John is not an A Student."

JOHN IS AN A STUDENT

[1]John's teachers enjoy having him in class. [2]He comes to class on time. [3]He listens intently to the instructor. [4]He wants to learn. [5]He passes all the tests. [6]His work habits evidence his sincerity. [7]He reads the assignments. [8]He completes his homework every night. [9]John listens to the laboratory tapes. [10]He does extra work. [11]He learns English rapidly. [12]Other students emulate his example. [13]John speaks only English on campus.

Assignment 6:B

Rewrite the following affirmative sentences as negative sentences. You will have to supply the hidden aux-word in some of the sentences. Your new title will be "Good Students."

BAD STUDENTS

[1]Robin and Terry are bad students. [2]They arrive in class late very often. [3]They sit in the back of the classroom. [4]They talk when they should be listening. [5]They sleep during the teacher's presentations. [6]Their notebooks are filled with doodles. [7]They do sloppy work. [8]They forget to do many assignments. [9]They misunderstand instructions. [10]They do things the wrong way. [11]They blame others when they have problems. [12]They complain about the work they have to do.

Assignment 6:C

Rewrite the following affirmative sentences as negative sentences. You will have to supply the hidden aux-word in some of the sentences.

MONEY

[1]Money is a necessary commodity. [2]People in all countries use it. [3]It is impossible to carry on trade without it. [4]Industry would come to a standstill without money. [5]Business would collapse. [6]Money needs to be regulated. [7]It is necessary to have banks to regulate money. [8]Financial institutions bring prosperity. [9]Bank failures cause hard times. [10]The world revolves fundamentally on bank credit. [11]Having an international currency seems desirable. [12]This would ensure world-wide prosperity.

7. VERB/AUX-WORD LOOK-ALIKES

7.1 Some aux-words and verbs look alike, but they do not have the same function or meaning. They should not be confused.

Aux-word		Verb	
Present	Past	Present	Past
do, does	did	do, does	did
have, has	had	have, has	had
can	could	can	canned
will	would	will	willed

7.2 Like all verbs, these verbs have hidden aux-words which must be used when making yes/no questions and negatives.

Examples:

John does his homework every day.	Does John do his homework every day? John doesn't do his homework every day.
John and Mary do their homework together.	Do John and Mary do their homework together? John and Mary don't do their homework together.
John did his homework last night.	Did John do his homework last night? John didn't do his homework last night.
John has a new car.	Does John have a new car? John doesn't have a new car.
John and Mary have a new car.	Do John and Mary have a new car? John and Mary don't have a new car.
John had an old car.	Did John have an old car? John didn't have an old car.
Mary cans tomatoes every summer.	Does Mary can tomatoes every summer? Mary doesn't can tomatoes every summer.
Mary canned tomatoes last summer.*	Did Mary can tomatoes last summer? Mary didn't can tomatoes last summer.
He willed his property to the Red Cross.**	Did he will his property to the Red Cross?

*The verb *can* means "preserve in cans or bottles."

**The verb *will* means "leave to someone or endow"—an older meaning of the verb *will* is *want*, e.g. The Lord's obedient children do what He wills. As a verb, *will* is rarely used in the present tense.

7.3 These verbs and aux-words may be used together.

Examples:

Do you do it this way?
He had had dinner before he came.
She can can fruit tomorrow.
He will will his money to us.

8. AUX-WORD MODALS

8.1 The aux-words *may, shall, will, must, might, should,* and *would* are often called modals. Although modals indicate time (present or past) like other aux-words and verbs, they also indicate:

1. time later than the tense expressed,
2. requests or permission,
3. ability or lack of ability,
4. obligation or duty, and
5. possibility.

8.2 Time Later than the Tense Expressed

Later time in the present is expressed by the modals *will* and *shall* (*is going to* and *are going to* also show later time in the present). That is, they are often used to express action after the present indicated time.

Examples:

I haven't read the book, but I shall read it.
I haven't read the book, but I will read it.
Shall we go tomorrow or right now?

(Some earlier grammars prescribed the use of *shall* with *I* and *we,* and *will* with other pronouns. *Shall* is currently used most of the time with questions.)

Later time in the past is expressed by the modal *would* (*was going to* and *were going to* also show later time in the past).

Example:

He said he hadn't read the book but he would read it.

Would is also used to express the habitual past.

Example:

When we were young we would swim every day during summer vacation.

(Later time is also explained in Chapter 6, Section 6.)

8.3 Requests

The modals *will, would,* and *could* are used in making requests. (*Can* is also used for requests in informal speech but is less acceptable in formal written English.)

Examples:

Will you help me?
Would you help me? (slightly more formal)
Could you help me?

8.4 Permission

The modal *may* is used to ask for or give permission. (*Can,* though frequently used for asking permission in speech, is unacceptable in formal written English.)

Examples:

May I leave?
You may leave now.

8.5 Ability

Can is used to indicate present ability.

Examples:

Bill can swim now. (Bill is able to swim now.)

Could is used to indicate past ability.

Example:

Bill couldn't swim last year. (Bill wasn't able to swim last year.)

8.6 Obligation or Duty

Should expresses strong obligation or duty (in the present or past).

Example:

Everyone who sings should join the choir.

Must expresses much stronger obligation or duty—really mandatory.

Example:

You must do your work or you will fail.

54 SENTENCE CONSTRUCTION

Should is also used when giving advice.

Example:
> You should exercise regularly.

Ought to and *had better* (informal) are often used in place of *should* to express obligation.

Examples:
> We ought to study more diligently.
> We had better study harder.

8.7 Possibility and Probability

The modals *may, might, should, must,* and *could* are used to indicate possibility or probability.

Examples:
> Something *may* turn up. I hope so anyway.
> Something *might* turn up. (less probability of the event happening)
> If he *should* come, tell him I left.
> If he's lived there that long, he *must* speak the language like a native. (a deduction)
> It *could* get cold here tonight.

8.8 This explanation of aux-words is necessarily general. Sometimes you may find aux-words used to express time and/or conditions other than those explained above. When combined with other aux-words, the meanings of these modals often change. These changes are explained in Chapter 6, Section 9.)

Assignment 8:A

Write the passage below and supply the appropriate aux-word in each of the blanks. There is more than one possible answer for some blanks.

LEARNING ENGLISH

[1]Many students learning English take classes so that they _____ learn to communicate in English.

[2]The teacher _____ help the students learn, but he or she _____ not learn for them. [3]Each student _____ do his own work. [4]He, himself, _____ learn to speak, read, and write English. [5]Some students _____ unaware of this fact, or if aware of it, forget it. [6]They _____ try anything to avoid doing their assignments. [7]They _____ say they want to learn English, but their actions _____ not support their words.

Assignment 8:B

Write the passage below and supply the appropriate aux-word in each of the blanks. There is more than one possible answer for some blanks.

HISTORY

[1]History _____ a fascinating subject. [2]Everyone _____ have a knowledge of history. [3]As you study history, you _____ learn many important things. [4]Understanding the

past _____ help you understand the present. ⁵A thorough knowledge of the past _____ even allow you to predict the future.

⁶The subject matter of history _____ as diverse as the people and places of the world. ⁷The study of history _____ the study of the foundation, growth, and decline of civilization. ⁸A complete historical view _____ include major intellectual, artistic, social, and spiritual contributions of the period and people studied.

⁹A general overview of world history _____ give you ideas of specific areas you _____ want to study. ¹⁰If you study one of these areas in depth you _____ become a specialist. ¹¹You _____ choose a specific time period or geographical area to study. ¹²You _____ specialize in medieval Europe. ¹³Polynesian history _____ interst you. ¹⁴You _____ be fascinated by ancient China. ¹⁵The history of many groups _____ never been written down. ¹⁶You _____ make a contribution to world knowledge.

¹⁷Whatever area or period you choose, you _____ need supporting skills to be a successful historian. ¹⁸The ability to read and write well in English and other languages _____ an important prerequisite to serious historical study.

Assignment 8:C

Write the passage below and supply the appropriate aux-word in each of the blanks. There is more than one possible answer for some blanks.

LATIN AMERICA

¹Latin America _____ a region filled with contrast and variety. ²Vast jungles, forbidding mountains, dry deserts, and endless plains _____ all part of its varied geograrphy. ³A broad variety of climatic conditions _____ be encountered in Latin America.

⁴Even in the area of language Latin America _____ diverse. ⁵All Latin Americans _____ not speak Spanish. ⁶Portuguese, French, Dutch, and English _____ some of the other languages spoken in the many different countries of Latin America.

⁷The countries of Latin America _____ not consider themselves similar. ⁸Rivalry between countries _____ not uncommon. ⁹Each country _____ developed its own solu-

56 SENTENCE CONSTRUCTION

tions to its problems. [10]Many different kinds of governments _____ be found in Latin America. [11]Both left-wing and right-wing dictatorships _____ found. [12]There _____ a growing middle ground in politics. [13]Stable, moderate governments _____ common. [14]The social middle class _____ also grown considerably in recent years.

[15]Rapid change _____ apparent throughout Latin America. [16]Busy ports and industrial centers _____ be seen in most Latin American countries. [17]Exports from Latin America are growing and _____ continue to grow in the future. [18]North Americans _____ understand this important part of the world better.

5
VERB FORMS AND THEIR USES

1. ENGLISH VERB FORMS

Refer to the chart below as you go through the following explanation of English verb forms.

ENGLISH VERB FORMS

Timeless forms			Time-included forms		
base form	*d-t-n* form	*-ing* form	+*s* form	No-*s* form	past form
go	gone	going	goes	go	went
eat	eaten	eating	eats	eat	ate
wait	waited	waiting	waits	wait	waited
look	looked	looking	looks	look	looked
break	broken	breaking	breaks	break	broke
put	put	putting	puts	put	put
read	read	reading	reads	read	read
work	worked	working	works	work	worked

1.1. All English verbs have six forms. Three of these forms include time—either past or present—and three are timeless.

Timeless forms   *Time-included forms*
base form   +*s* form
d-t-n form   no-*s* form
-ing form   past form

1.2. The **base form** of a verb is called the base form because other verb forms are made from it. The base form is the form found in the dictionary. Usually the dictionary shows the other forms of a verb only when they are irregular forms.

1.3 The *d-t-n* form is called the *d-t-n* form because it almost always ends in the letter *d, t,* or *n.* (It is sometimes called the "past participle.")

The *d-t-n* form of regular verbs is formed by adding *ed* to the base form. If the base form ends with the letter *e,* only the *d* is added.

Examples:

    base form   *d-t-n form*
    walk   walked
    create   created

The *d-t-n* forms of irregular verbs often end in *n* or *t*. Some have different forms.

Examples:

base form	d-t-n form
give	given
leave	left

A few irregular verbs are gradually becoming regular and may have two *d-t-n* forms. Either form is correct.

Examples:

base form	d-t-n forms
dream	dreamt or dreamed
prove	proven or proved

Spelling note: The spelling rules given for the past ending *-ed* in section 1.7 of this chapter apply to the *d-t-n* form also.

1.4 The *-ing* form always ends in *-ing*. (It is sometimes called the "present participle.") It is usually formed by simply adding *-ing* to the base form. However, there are some exceptions to this rule.

Verbs ending with a consonant preceded by any vowel except *w* usually double the final consonant when adding *-ing*.

Example:

base form	-ing form
hop	hopping

Verbs ending is an unpronounced *e* usually drop the *e* before adding *-ing*.

Example:

base form	-ing form
hope	hoping

One-syllable base forms which end in *-ie* substitute *y* for *ie* before the *-ing* is added.

Example:

base form	-ing form
die	dying

1.5 The +*s* form is called the +*s* form because it ends in the letter *s*. It is usually formed by adding *s* to the base form. However, there are some exceptions.

Base forms which end in the letter *y* preceded by a consonant drop the *y* and add *-ies*.

Example:

base form	+s form
try	tries

Base forms which end in the letter *y* preceded by a vowel simply add *-s*.

Example:

base form	+s form
play	plays

Base forms which end in *-s, -sh, -ch, -z*, or *-x* add *-es*.

Examples:

base form	+s form
miss	misses
wish	wishes
catch	catches
buzz	buzzes
fix	fixes

1.6 The no-*s* form and the base form look alike. However, although these forms are spelled and pronounced the same way, they are considered separate verb forms because they are used differently. Each form has a distinct function.

1.7 The past forms of regular verbs end in *-ed*. If the base form ends with the letter *e*, only the *d* is added.

Examples:

base form	past form
finish	finished
complete	completed

Verbs ending in *y* usually change the *y* to *i* and then add *-ed*.

Example:

base form	past form
cry	cried

When the final *y* is preceded by a vowel, it does not change to *i*.

Example:

base form	past form
play	played

Regular verbs ending in a single vowel and consonant often double the final consonant and then add *-ed*.

Example:

base form	past form
occur	occurred

Some exceptions to this rule are:

1. Verbs of more than one syllable which are not accented on the last syllable do not double the final consonant.

Example:

base form	past form
remember	remembered

2. Verbs that end in the letter *w* do not double the *w*. They only add *-ed*.

Example:

base form	past form
stew	stewed

Many of the most commonly used verbs have irregular past forms. Appendix C (pages 154–155) lists many of these irregular verbs.

The past form and *d-t-n* form of some verbs look alike. However, although these forms are spelled and pronounced the same way, they are considered separate verb forms because they are used differently. Each form has a distinct function.

Assignment 1:A

On the chart below, one of the six forms of each of a number of English verbs has been supplied. Copy this chart and complete it by writing the other five forms in the appropriate spaces.

TIMELESS FORMS			TIME-INCLUDED FORMS		
base form	*d-t-n* form	*-ing* form	+*s* form	no-*s* form	past form
		doing			
	gone				
fly					
					ate
				sleep	
fall					
			thinks		
	felt				
		choosing			
					knew

Assignment 1:B

On the chart below, one of the six forms of each of a number of English verbs has been supplied. Copy this chart and complete it by writing the other five forms in the appropriate spaces.

TIMELESS FORMS			TIME-INCLUDED FORMS		
base form	*d-t-n* form	*-ing* form	+*s* form	no-*s* form	past form
rise					
		writing			
			gives		
				become	
keep					
	said				
					found
		losing			
			reads		
come					

Assignment 1:C

On the chart below, one of the six forms of each of a number of English verbs has been supplied. Copy this chart and complete it by writing the other five forms in the appropriate spaces.

TIMELESS FORMS			TIME-INCLUDED FORMS		
base form	*d-t-n* form	*-ing* form	+*s* form	no-*s* form	past form
			begins		
		speaking			
				take	
drive					
				bring	
		buying			
	kept				
					saw
tell					
					studied

2. PRESENT TIME-INCLUDED FORMS AND THEIR USES

This explanation is limited to subject/verb agreement. An explanation of the use of time-included forms in relation to time is given in the next chapter.

2.1 The present tense has two verb forms—the **+s** and the **no-s**.

The **+s** form is used with **singular** subjects (except the pronouns *I* and *you*).

Examples:
    Richard always completes his homework.
    He sometimes stays up late to finish it.
    He never comes to class without it.

The **no-s** form is used with **plural** subjects (and the pronouns *I* and *you*).

Examples:
    George and Bill never complete their homework.
    They always stay up late watching television.
    They often sleep in class.

    I sometimes forget to do my homework.
    I usually finish it early.

    You help yourself when you do your homework carefully.
    You hurt yourself when you do it carelessly.

62 SENTENCE CONSTRUCTION

2.2 Singular subjects followed by words or phrases such as *as well as, along with, together with, with,* or *like* remain **singular** although the nouns which follow them may be plural.

Examples:

Mary, along with her friends, is coming tonight.
The teacher, together with the students, works hard.
Joe, with his parents, watches TV every night.

2.3 The expression *one of* is always followed by a **plural** count noun. Because *one* is singular, this expression is followed by the **+s** form of the verb or aux-word.

Examples:

One of the books has a page missing.
One of the players was injured during the game.

2.4 The terms *everyone, everybody, no one, nobody, anyone,* and *anybody* are **singular,** although they may refer to more than one person. For this reason, they are followed by the **+s** form of the verb or aux-word.

Examples:

Everyone likes Joe.
Nobody hates him.
Everybody likes a party.
Anybody knows that.

Assignment 2:A

Write the following passage, replacing each of the blanks with the correct form (+s or no-s) of the verb indicated beneath each blank. The first one has been done for you.

SURGERY

¹Surgery _seems_ to be a highly complicated procedure. ²A surgeon, with assistants,
         seem

_____ well in advance for specialized operations. ³One of the nurses _____ the
    plan   supervise

instruments. ⁴The anesthesiologist, with an assistant or several assistants, _____ specific duties.
                                                                                    have

⁵Blood pressure _____ monitoring. ⁶They _____ respiratory action and
                      need   watch

_____ all life signs. ⁷Interns or a nurse _____ ready to assist. ⁸One of the
     check   stand

nurses _____ watching as the surgeon or the assisting doctors _____ up to see
           keep   scrub

that no one _____ to wash his hands for the required time and that everyone _____
                fail   remain

uncontaminated before the operation _____ . ⁹Everybody _____ to take the
                                           begin   need

utmost care to see that everything _____ sterile in the operating room.
                                          remain

Assignment 2:B

Write the following passage, replacing each of the blanks with the correct form (+s or no-s) of the verb indicated beneath each blank. The first one has been done for you.

ICE

¹The polar ice pack *presents* (present) a formidable barrier to shipping. ²In some years the ice pack _____ (remain) solid, and the northwest passage _____ (fail) to open as a seagoing lane. ³Ice breakers _____ (try) in vain to push aside the solid ice. ⁴An ice breaker, though strong and powerful, sometimes _____ (become) frozen in the ice.

⁵In other years when the passage opens, large icebergs _____ (float) southward and _____ (menace) shipping in the Atlantic Ocean. ⁶A single berg or ice floe _____ (weigh) thousands of tons and _____ (melt) slowly in the frigid water. ⁷An iceberg with its huge underwater bulk _____ (jam) against the shore or _____ (grind) against other bergs. ⁸Grinding ice _____ (crush) strong boats like matchsticks, and icebergs _____ (create) hazards at sea. ⁹Everyone _____ (know) the story of the Titanic and no one _____ (care) to share that fate.

Assignment 2:C

Write the following passage, replacing each of the blanks with the correct form (+s or no-s) of the verb indicated beneath each blank. The first one has been done for you.

STARTING A BUSINESS

¹Richard, with his brothers, *wants* (want) to start his own business. ²Neither his parents nor his friends _____ (think) he can succeed. ³Even a small business _____ (need) stock and equipment, and of course it also _____ (require) money to run until it _____ (start) to make a profit. ⁴Creditors _____ (demand) prompt payment. ⁵They _____ (charge) interest. ⁶The government _____ (demand) accurate bookkeeping. ⁷Even small businesses _____ (have) countless forms to fill out quarterly. ⁸Legible reports _____ (take) time to fill out properly. ⁹In business, time _____ (mean) money. ¹⁰Insurance on property and goods _____ (pose) another financial problem. ¹¹Richard's father thinks Richard and his brothers _____ (need) to forget the idea. ¹²Their present jobs _____ (pay) them an adequate income. ¹³His friends _____ (feel) the same way.

3. PAST TIME-INCLUDED FORMS AND THEIR USES

3.1 Every English verb has only one past tense form. It makes no difference whether the subject is singular or plural.

Examples:

The car crashed.
The cars crashed.

He went to town yesterday.
They went to town yesterday.

Assignment 3:A

Rewrite the paragraph below in the past tense. Add Yesterday *at the beginning of the first sentence and make all the other necessary changes in verb forms. Be sure to eliminate the time expressions that indicate the use of the present tense—*usually, frequently, often, *and* sometimes.

MARY'S DAY

[1]Mary usually gets up at 6:00 a.m. [2]She takes a shower, gets dressed, and then fixes her breakfast. [3]While she eats breakfast, she listens to the morning news broadcast. [4]Mary rides to work on the bus and arrives at the office about eight o'clock. [5]She frequently works without a break until 11:30. [6]Then she takes an hour for lunch. [7]She eats a sandwich which she takes with her so she has time to go shopping. [8]Mary returns to the office at 12:30 and works until four o'clock. [9]However, she takes a half-hour break at two o'clock. [10]Mary takes the bus home again, but often stops for dinner at a small restaurant near her home. [11]She sometimes has a date for the evening and gets home tired but happy around midnight.

Assignment 3:B

Rewrite the paragraph below in the past tense. Change Here stands *to* There stood *and make all the other necessary changes in verb forms.*

MAKING A MOVIE

[1]Here stands a Hollywood movie set. [2]Cameras grind away as the action begins. [3]Heroes, heroines, and villains share the spotlight. [4]Each tries to capture the limelight. [5]None of them really succeeds. [6]Painted backdrops and a false-fronted house serve as a background for the scenes. [7]A stunt man leaps into action as the star hides in the shadows ready to stand at the side of the recently rescued heroine. [8]The villain and the hero trade punches which fall short of their mark, although the men stagger and fall as though struck. [9]The film records the action as each actor or actress acts passionately for the faithful moviegoers who enjoy the vicarious thrills of another Western.

Assignment 3:C

Rewrite the paragraph below in the past tense. Add When I was young, *to the beginning of the first sentence. Make all the other necessary changes in verb forms.*

FADS AND FASHIONS

[1]Fads and fashions come and go. [2]Men's and women's clothes change with the season and the year. [3]People dress for fashion rather than comfort. [4]When stylish, feet—broad or narrow, short-toed or long-toed—crowd into narrow, pointed shoes. [5]Hard, inflexible wooden slabs become fashionable and replace soft leather shoes, not on country lanes and cobblestone roads but on city streets and hardwood floors.

[6]Fashion dictates the food people eat as well. [7]One year, refined foods replace natural foods. [8]The next, cooked foods supplant raw ones. [9]Fads and fashion support change. [10]New things replace old ones. [11]Then the cycle starts again.

Assignment 3.1:A

Rewrite the following paragraph in the past tense. Change the first sentence to I used to be a teacher. *When necessary, change the verbs and aux-words in the other sentences to past forms.*

A TEACHER'S DREAM

¹I am a teacher. ²I love my professional life. ³I can scarcely wait to get to my classroom. ⁴The students all come to class early. ⁵They have written all their homework carefully and neatly. ⁶They are prepared for the day's work. ⁷Everyone listens intently as I give the lecture. ⁸No one whispers or is inattentive. ⁹The questions that are asked are intelligent and thought-provoking. ¹⁰I always know the answers and the students are delighted to learn more about the subject. ¹¹The students hate to leave so they linger after class is over because they want to know more. ¹²Between classes they diligently go to the library to do research on the subjects we are studying. ¹³The students and I look forward to the discussions we will have during the next class period. ¹⁴Turning in grades becomes an easy task with students like these who study for knowledge and care very little about report cards.

Assignment 3.1:B

Rewrite the following paragraph in the past tense. Put Last year, *at the beginning of the first sentence. When necessary, change the verbs and aux-words in the other sentences to past forms.*

A PROFESSIONAL GOLFER

¹John Jones plays golf to make money. ²He is a professional golfer. ³This seems like an easy and pleasant life. ⁴However, this is not the case. ⁵He is away from his family most of the year. ⁶If he drops out of the professional tour he can't make a living. ⁷Even then, unless he has a sponsor, in a bad year his living depends on his earlier winnings which he has saved. ⁸Constant practice is necessary as he has to stay in top physical condition. ⁹His competition never lets up. ¹⁰One bad stroke will put him out of the money. ¹¹The crowd, which follows the golfers around the course, constantly praises or boos him. ¹²Jones, along with his caddy, ignores the crowd if he expects to finish in the money. ¹³Although golfer Jones's winnings may be high or low, expenses remain fixed. ¹⁴Professional fees have to be paid before he enters a tournament. ¹⁵It costs him a lot of money to travel, as the tournaments are held in different sections of the United States and many occur in other countries. ¹⁶Hotel and food bills take a sizable sum. ¹⁷Added to this is the cost of expensive equipment—clubs, balls, etc. ¹⁸John Jones, like many other pros, plays professional golf to establish a name so he can quit, stay home, and really make money advertising sports equipment on TV.

Assignment 3.1:C

Rewrite the following paragraph in the past tense. Change the first sentence to When I saw him last year, Roger had a new job. *When necessary, change the verbs and aux-words in the other sentences to past forms.*

A NEW JOB

¹Roger has a new job. ²He is very happy with it. ³He can come and go as he pleases. ⁴He drives a company car to and from work. ⁵He meets many interesting people as he travels throughout the country. ⁶His company pays his hotel and food bills when he is away from home. ⁷Above all, the pay is good. ⁸He is thinking of taking a correspondence course so he can learn more about business procedures and bookkeeping. ⁹Possibly this will lead to an even better position. ¹⁰There are lots of possibilities for advancement in his company.

4. TIMELESS VERB FORMS AND THEIR USES

Refer to the chart below as you go through the following explanation of how English verb forms are used. This explanation is limited to aux-word/verb combinations and agreement between subjects and aux-words. An explanation of the use of aux-words and verbs in relation to time is given in chapter 6.

ENGLISH VERB FORMS

TIMELESS FORMS			TIME-INCLUDED FORMS		
base form	*d-t-n* form	*-ing* form	+*s* form	No-*s* form	past form
go	gone	going	goes	go	went
eat	eaten	eating	eats	eat	ate
wait	waited	waiting	waits	wait	waited
look	looked	looking	looks	look	looked
break	broken	breaking	breaks	break	broke
put	put	putting	puts	put	put
read	read	reading	reads	read	read
work	worked	working	works	work	worked
↑	↑	↑	↑	↑	↑

present	past	present	past	present	past			
will	would	have	had	is/am	was	(does)	(do)	(did)
can	could	has		are	were			
do/does	did							
shall	should	base	-*ing*	base	*d-t-n*	-*ing*		
may	might	have	having	be	been	being		
must								
AUX-WORDS						HIDDEN AUX-WORDS		

4.1 The verb form used with an aux-word must be one of the three timeless forms (*base*, *d-t-n*, or -*ing*). These verb forms do not indicate time; the aux-word does. When used as verbs, all timeless verb forms are preceded by an aux-word.

4.2 The **base** form of a verb is usually preceded by a **modal** aux-word.

Examples:

I *will go*.   He *will work*.
  aux base   aux base

When the function word *to* precedes the base form, the resulting combination (often called the infinitive) is used as a noun. This is explained in Chapter 13, Section 4.

The **base form** is also used following other verbs such as *have to*, *ought to* (which acts like an aux-word in questions and negatives) and *used to* and in most other places where a verb form follows *to*.

Examples:

We ought to attend the assembly.   (*ought to* indicates present obligation; *ought to* has no past form)

I have to leave tonight.   (*have to* or *had to* indicates necessity)
I had to leave early last night.

I used to make a lot of money.   (*used to* indicates habitual past; *used to* has no present form)

The **base form** follows the object of certain verbs, such as *let, make,* and *hear.* In this case, the base form indicates the action of the object.

Examples:
>My father won't *let* me *go.*
>She *made* my brother *work.*
>I have *heard* her *tell* that story many times.

4.3 The **d-t-n form,** in a basic sentence, is always preceded by the aux-words which are forms of *have.*

Examples:
>I *have* gone.
>   aux   d-t-n
>He *has* worked.
>   aux   d-t-n

In the passive transformation (this is explained in Chapter 9) the *d-t-n* form follows a form of the aux-word *be.*

The *d-t-n* form may also be used as a **modifier** (this is explained in Chapters 8 and 12). In this case it does not function as a verb and needs no aux-word.

4.4 The **-ing form,** when used as a verb, follows the aux-words which are forms of *be.*

Examples:
>I *am*   going.
>   aux   -ing
>He *is* working.
>   aux   -ing

When the *-ing* form is used as a **modifier** (this is explained in Chapters 8 and 12), no aux-word is used.

When the *-ing* form is used to begin a **noun phrase** (this is explained in Chapter 13), it is not accompanied by an aux-word.

4.5 All aux-words except the modals have **timeless forms** which function the same way that timeless verb forms do. The **base** forms of these aux-words, *have* or *be,* follow modals. The **d-t-n** form *been* follows a form of *have* (except in the passive transformation). The **-ing** form *being* is used after some other form of *be.* The **-ing** form *having* is used only in half-sentences (these forms are explained in Chapter 12).

Examples:

Subject	Modal	*have*	*be*		Remainder of sentence
He	could	have	been		in the accident.
		base	d-t-n		
He			is	being	funny.
				-ing	
He	will		be		leaving soon.
			base		

4.6 The three time-included verb forms (+s, no-s, and past) contain the **hidden aux-words** *does, do,* and *did.* When these hidden aux-words are taken out and used to form negatives, to form yes/no questions, or for emphasis, the time-included forms change to the timeless base form of the verb. (This is explained in Chapter 4.)

Examples:

	He	<u>likes</u> detective stories.	(statement)
		+s	
<u>Does</u>	he	<u>like</u> detective stories?	(yes/no question)
aux		base	
	He	doesn't <u>like</u> detective stories.	(negative statement)
		aux base	
	His parents	<u>like</u> detective stories.	(statement)
		no-s	
<u>Do</u>	his parents	<u>like</u> detective stories?	(yes/no question)
aux		base	
	His parents	don't <u>like</u> detective stories.	(negative statement)
		aux base	

Assignment 4:A

*Write the passage below, supplying the correct timeless form (*base, d-t-n, *or* -ing*) of the verb indicated beneath each blank.*

TONGUE TWISTERS

[1] Repetitive sounds have _____ (form) the basis for riddles, puns, and tongue twisters in all languages. [2] They must _____ (be) said aloud or they can't _____ (be) fully appreciated. [3] If one repeats any combination of sounds often enough and fast enough, the sounds will _____ (become) strange sounding or distorted. [4] Two similar sounds which have _____ (be) placed together are often confused. [5] Probably the sibilants, or hissing sounds, in English have _____ (produce) the majority of tongue twisters, although "Peter Piper and his pickled peppers" has always _____ (be) popular. [6] Children have _____ (have) fun with the relatively easy "She sells seashells by the seashore," while adults will usually _____ (try) the more sophisticated "The sixth sick sheik's sixth sheep's sick." [7] You might _____ (like) to find a book and try a few English tongue twisters. [8] You should _____ (plan) on lots of practice. [9] After you have _____ (spend) a lot of time and can _____ (repeat) them easily and perfectly, you might _____ (impress) your friends with your linguistic ability.

Assignment 4:B

*Write the passage below, supplying the correct timeless form (*base, d-t-n, *or* -ing*) of the verb indicated beneath each blank.*

EARTHQUAKES

¹A recent earthquake has _____ the lives of over twenty thousand people. ²Thousands more
                take
have been _____ without homes and family. ³Although scientists have _____
     leave   locate
earthquake-prone places, anywhere in the world the earth could _____ to shake at any moment.
                                                                                    start
⁴The tremor might _____, or _____ to shake until buildings have _____
                    subside   continue   topple
and people have been killed and hurt.

⁵Earthquakes have long _____ one of nature's most curious phenomena. ⁶So far, only
                                   be
astrologers or other pseudo-scientists have _____ to _____ the specific location
                                          attempt   predict
or time of an earthquake. ⁷However, scientists are _____ to find a way to _____
                                                 try   predict
earthquakes. ⁸They are _____ the slightest bulge in the earth's surface in earthquake-prone
                    measure
places. ⁹They have _____ and _____ many of the faults where buckling has
                 chart   name
_____. ¹⁰Hopefully, before too long scientists will _____ to predict tremors
 occur   learn
so people can leave these places temporarily and avoid much death and suffering.

Assignment 4:C

*Write the passage below, supplying the correct timeless form (*base, d-t-n, *or* -ing*) of the verb indicated beneath each blank. Remember, the* -ing *form follows prepositions.*

READ THE LABEL

¹Many people have never _____ or _____ to _____ the labels
                             learn   bother   read
on the packages or cans of food they buy daily. ²By just _____ at the pictures on a container
                                                           look
one doesn't _____ very much about the product. ³By law, all packaged food must _____
            learn   list
the contents of the container. ⁴This list will _____ the preservatives as well as the main ingredients.
                                                             include
⁵People can _____ illness by _____ if anything they have _____
              prevent   see   find
that they are allergic to is included. ⁶They can _____ malnutrition by _____
                                                 avoid   select
preparations to which essential vitamins and minerals have _____ added. ⁷One should
                                                                 be

_____ the order of the ingredients on the label since it indicates the relative amount of each
   notice

ingredient. ⁸The most common ingredient must _____ first on the list. ⁹A consumer should
                                                               appear

_____ knowledgeable about labels. ¹⁰One can _____ money and _____
  become   save   have

better health by _____ them carefully.
                examine

5. MULTIPLE AUX-WORD/VERB COMBINATIONS

More than one aux-word can be used at a time. When this is done, only the first aux-word shows time. The aux-words which follow must be timeless forms.

The aux-words below are called **modals**:

can (can't)	could (couldn't)
may (mayn't)	might (mightn't)
shall (shan't)	should (shouldn't)
will (won't)	would (wouldn't)
may (mayn't)	must (mustn't)

Modals do **not** have timeless forms. Therefore, only one of them can be used in an aux-word/verb group and it must come first in the group.

The other aux-words (*have, has, had, is, am, are, was,* and *were*) have **timeless** forms as follows:

Base	d-t-n	-ing
be	been	being
have		(having)

These timeless forms have a definite order and follow the basic rules for verbs:

    base forms (*have* and *be*) follow the modals (or their negative forms),

    the **d-t-n** form (*been*) follows any form of *have,*

    the **-ing** form (*being*) follows any form of *be,* and

    the **-ing** form (*having*) is used only when making half-sentences (this is explained in Chapter 12).

The "Order of Auxiliaries and Verbs" chart below shows all the possible aux-word/verb form combinations in English, including those used in the passive transformation (which is explained in Chapter 9).

ORDER OF AUXILIARIES AND VERBS

	MODAL	HAVE	BE	BE (passive)	VERB FORM
1.					-s, no-s, past
2.	modal				base
3.	modal	have			d-t-n
4.	modal		be		-ing
5.	modal			be	d-t-n
6.	modal	have	been		-ing
7.	modal	have		been	d-t-n
8.	modal		be	being	d-t-n
9.*	modal	have	been	being	d-t-n
10.		have, has, had			d-t-n
11.		have, has, had	been		-ing
12.		have, has, had		been	d-t-n
13.*		have, has, had	been	being	d-t-n
14.			is, am, are, was, were		-ing
15.			is, am, are, was, were	being	d-t-n
16.				is, am, are, was, were	d-t-n

Example sentences:
1. He studies the lesson. They study the lesson. We studied the lesson.
2. He should study the lesson. He can't study the lesson.
3. He might have studied the lesson. He couldn't have studied the lesson.
4. He must be studying the lesson. He should be studying the lesson.
5. The lesson should be studied (by him).
6. He should have been studying (the lesson).
7. The lesson should have been studied (by him).
8. The lesson might be being studied (by him).
9.* The lesson could have been being studied (by him).
10. He has studied the lesson.
11. He has been studying the lesson.
12. The lesson has been studied (by him).
13.* The lesson has been being studied (by him).
14. He is studying the lesson.
15. The lesson is being studied (by him).
16. The lesson is studied (by him).

*rarely, if ever, used

72 SENTENCE CONSTRUCTION

Assignment 5:A

Copy the paragraph below and circle the aux-words which show time. Underline the timeless verb forms and timeless aux-word forms.

GUILTY OR NOT GUILTY

[1] Sometimes people have been found guilty of crimes they did not commit. [2] Some convicted non-criminals have been confined for many years before they have been freed. [3] They should never have been put in jail, but juries and judges have not always been blessed with the ability to judge correctly. [4] At the first trial, facts may have been withheld, or witnesses might not have told the truth. [5] In any event, sometimes people will have been judged guilty and may have had to pay the penalty for a crime which they have not committed.

Assignment 5:B

Copy the paragraph below and circle the aux-words which show time. Underline the timeless verb forms and timeless aux-word forms.

POLLUTION

[1] Up until the past few years, government bureaus and the general public have not been concerned with the earth's physical condition. [2] Today's world might have been in better shape if this had not been the case. [3] Prevention has always been less costly than restoration. [4] If people would have had the necessary prevention foresight, it might have been possible to have avoided today's pollution problems. [5] Because they did not have the vision, however, we must not only restore that which has been lost, but we will also need to plan wisely so that that which we have now will not have been destroyed as well. [6] The world can be cleaned up, but we must start now.

Assignment 5:C

Copy the paragraph below and circle the aux-words which show time. Underline the timeless verb forms and timeless aux-word forms.

SIGNING A CONTRACT

[1] People have frequently been heard to say that they should have been thinking more clearly when they signed a contract to buy something. [2] At one time, to honor the contract and pay up was all that a person could do. [3] Under the Uniform Commercial Code, the United States government has been protecting people who might have been talked into some project or proposition. [4] Under a new law, consumers may have up to three days to change their minds about purchases they have signed for. [5] Instead of having to honor the contract and saying they should have known better, they may cancel the contract without any penalty. [6] Many people think this law should have been enacted years earlier.

6. TWO-WORD VERBS

6.1 A **two-word verb** is different in use and meaning from a **verb followed by a preposition**.

The second word of a two-word verb (the particle) is an essential part of the verb itself. Removing it changes the meaning of the verb.

The **particle** (second word) of a two-word verb does not always show location or direction, although it may.

The **preposition** following a verb shows location or direction.

6.2 There are a number of ways to distinguish a two-word verb from a verb followed by a preposition. The following two tests may be helpful.

1. Divide the sentence in half between the verb and the preposition or particle. Move the last half of the sentence in front of the subject. If the resulting sentence still makes sense and is acceptable English, then you have divided a verb-preposition combination.

Example:

George ran / up a hill. (verb followed by a preposition)
Up a hill George ran. (acceptable)

If the resulting sentence does *not* make sense, has a different meaning, or is not acceptable English, then you have divided a two-word verb (which should *not* be divided this way).

Example:

George ran / up a large bill. (two-word verb = accumulated)
Up a large bill George ran. (unacceptable)

2. Very often, a single-word verb can be substituted for a two-word verb without changing the meaning. (Notice that this substitution often increases the level of formality of the sentence.)

Examples:

Alexander looked over the used car. (two-word verb)
Alexander examined the used car. (single-word verb substitute)

Alexander looked over the fence. (verb + preposition)
(There is no single-word substitute for *look over* in this sentence.)

A list of some common two-word verbs and their single-word verb counterparts can be found in Appendix D.

6.3 Some two-word verbs become three-word verbs (by adding a second particle) when they have a direct object.

Example:

Joe got out. (two-word verb)
Joe got out of the difficult situation. (three-word verb)

Assignment 6:A

In the story below, the verbs followed by particles (two-word verbs) or prepositions have been italicized. On your paper, by sentence number, list only the two-word verbs.

JOHN'S CAR

[1]The minute John *got up* this morning, he *ran out* to the garage behind his house. [2]He *opened up* his toolbox and began to *work on* his car. [3]He was trying to *figure out* why his car wouldn't *start up*. [4]He *looked at* everything, but he couldn't *pin down* the reason. [5]He *filled up* the gas tank, *checked under* the hood, *tuned up* the engine, *hooked up* a loose wire, and even *took apart* the carburetor. [6]He tried everything he could *think of,* but the car still wouldn't *start up*. [7]He finally *gave up*.

[8]To take his mind *off* the car, John *went in* the house, *sat down on* the couch and *turned on* the television. [9]That didn't *help him out,* though. [10]A do-it-yourself auto-mechanic program was on. [11]He *watched it for* a few minutes until he *came up with* an idea of what might be wrong with his car. [12]Then he *went out* and started *working on* it again.

74   SENTENCE CONSTRUCTION

Assignment 6:B

In the story below, the verbs followed by particles (two-word verbs) or prepositions have been italicized. On your paper, by sentence number, list only the two-word verbs.

A FRIEND IN NEED

[1] The other morning, just after I *woke up,* my friend Harry *called* me *up* and asked me to *hurry over* to his place. [2] It seemed that he and his girlfriend had *broken up* the night before, and he was feeling really sad. [3] Well, I *hurried up* and *gobbled down* my breakfast and *ran out* of the house. [4] I *hopped in* my old car and turned the key, but nothing happened. [5] It wouldn't even *turn over.* [6] I had *left* the lights *on* overnight, and the battery had *run down.* [7] It was completely dead. [8] Nevertheless, a friend in need is a friend indeed, so I *jumped on* my brother's motorcycle and *started over* to Harry's house. [9] Our neighbor's dog, which hates me, saw its chance and *ran out* furiously. [10] *Chasing after* me, with one big bite it *took* a big piece *out* of my pants. [11] However, that didn't stop me, and I *continued on.* [12] A few blocks down the road I *ran out* of gas. [13] I *jumped off* and *ran to* the corner gas station. [14] I had to *put* the gas *in* a can and then *run back* to the motorcycle. [15] Finally, I *pulled up* in front of Harry's house. [16] I *hopped off* the motorcycle and *ran up* to the front door and *knocked on* it. [17] Harry's mother *came out* and said, "Oh, Harry isn't here." [18] Just after I had *hung up* the phone, he had *called* his girlfriend *up.* [19] They had *made up* over the phone and Harry had *gone over* to see her.

Assignment 6:C

In the story below, the verbs followed by particles (two-word verbs) or prepositions have been italicized. On your paper, by sentence number, list only the two-word verbs.

AN ORDERLY CLASSROOM

[1] In an orderly classroom everything works smoothly. [2] When the students *come into* the classroom they *hand in* their homework. [3] The students' notebooks are organized so they don't have to waste time *looking for* their homework assignments. [4] They *sit* quietly *at* their desks. [5] The teacher *hands out* their papers which have been corrected. [6] When the teacher tells the students to *open up* their books, they *turn to* the right page and *look over* the lesson together. [7] The students don't whisper and *talk to* each other. [8] No one has to *wake up* sleeping students. [9] There are no inattentive or lazy students who *fall behind* and have to *catch up* later. [10] As the teacher talks, the students *take down* orderly notes so that if they have a question later they can *look up* the answer and find it. [11] As students *think of* questions, they ask them to the teacher. [12] No one speaks without *putting up* his hand and *waiting for* the teacher to *call on* him. [13] At the end of the class period, the teacher *hands out* the assignment for the next day and the students *stand up* and *go out* the door. [14] The teacher *picks up* any papers that have been *dropped on* the floor or any books that have been *left behind,* erases the blackboard, and *turns off* the lights before leaving.

7. SEPARABLE AND INSEPARABLE TWO-WORD VERBS

7.1   There are two kinds of two-word verbs, **separable** and **inseparable**. The two-word verbs included in Appendix D, page 156, are divided into these two categories.

7.2   An object cannot be placed between the verb and the particle of an **inseparable** two-word verb.

Examples:

The teacher **called on** the students.
The teacher **called** the students **on**. (unacceptable)

My mother **looked for** my brother.
My mother **looked** my brother **for**. (unacceptable)

(An object cannot be placed between a verb and *preposition* either.)

7.3 An object **may** be placed between the verb and the particle of a **separable** two-word verb. It may also occur after the particle. Either position is acceptable.

Examples:

    Susan **called up** John.
    Susan **called** John **up.** (both acceptable)

    Mr. Garcia **filled out** the form.
    Mr. Garcia **filled** the form **out.** (both acceptable)

7.4 When the object of a **separable** two-word verb is a **pronoun,** it **must** be placed **between** the verb and the particle.

Examples:

    The pilot **tried out** the new airplane.
    The pilot **tried** it **out.** (acceptable)
    The pilot **tried out** it. (unacceptable)

Assignment 7:A

Answer the following questions in the affirmative, *using complete sentences (long answers). Use appropriate pronouns in your answers whenever possible. The first one has been done for you.*

STUDYING

1. Did you go over your in-class notes after class yesterday?

    Yes, I went over them.

2. Did you mix up the assignments made by the teacher?

3. Did you try to get out of doing your homework?

4. Did you put off doing your homework last night?

5. Did you finally get around to doing your homework?

6. Did you get through with your homework before midnight?

7. Did you look up the unfamiliar words in the dictionary?

8. Did you show up to class on time today?

76 SENTENCE CONSTRUCTION

9. Did you hand in your homework when the teacher asked for it?

10. Did you think of a good essay topic to write on in class?

11. Did you use up all your notebook paper writing?

12. Did you leave out any important punctuation marks?

13. Did you go over your essay to check it for mistakes?

14. Did you do over the parts that were wrong?

15. Did you talk over your problems with your teacher?

Assignment 7:B

Answer the following questions in the affirmative, *using complete sentences (long answers). Use appropriate pronouns* in your answers whenever possible.

TODAY'S ACTIVITIES

1. Did you get up early this morning?

2. Did you make up a list of things to do today?

3. Did you keep up with your schedule?

4. Did you wait for help from someone else?

5. Did you wade into your work alone?

6. Did you clean up your room?

7. Did you take out the trash?

8. Did you put away your things?

9. Did you pick up the mail?

10. Did you keep on working even when you were tired?

11. Did you look for ways to make your work more pleasant?

12. Did you get through with what you planned to do?

13. Did you run out of energy by the end of the day?

14. Did you make up your mind to do things differently tomorrow?

15. Did you turn off all the lights before going to bed?

Assignment 7:C

Answer the following questions in the affirmative, *using complete sentences (long answers). Use appropriate* pronouns *in your answers whenever possible.*

HARRY'S TROUBLED LIFE

1. Did Harry get into trouble early in life?

2. Did he fool around in school?

3. Did he fall behind his classmates?

4. Did he get into fights often?

5. Did he drop out of school as soon as he could?

6. Did he fall in with bad company out of school?

7. Did he pick up bad habits and ideas from his new friends?

8. Did he take part in a number of robberies?

9. Did he later hold up a bank by himself?

10. Did he blow open the safe?

11. Did he get away with robbery the first few times?

12. Did the law finally catch up with Harry?

13. Did he finally wake up?

14. Did he make up his mind to go straight?

15. Did he clean up his life?

6
VERBS AND TIME

1. ESTABLISHING TIME

1.1 Time and tense are not synonyms—that is, they do not always mean the same thing.

In this book, we define tense as the inflection or changing of an aux-word or verb form in connection with time.

We can write about many different times, but we use only two tenses—present or past. (In Chapter 5 it is established that aux-words and verbs have only three time-included forms—two present forms and one past form. The other forms are timeless. See the chart on page 57.)

1.2 Time (present or past) is established by

1. **a time expression,**

Examples:

yesterday, last week, right now, on Monday, etc. (The verb tense must agree with the time indicated by the time expression.)

and/or
2. **the aux-word or verb itself.**

Examples:

John goes, John went;   I can go, I could go

In writing, once the time is established, it should **not** be changed without **a signal** (a time expression),

Example:

Yesterday, I *had* many things to do, but *today* I *have* a lot of free time.
(past)   (past)   (present) (present)

and/or **a valid reason.**

Example:

When we *saw* the sunrise, we *knew* we *were* facing east because the sun always *comes* up in the east.
(past)   (past)   (past)   (present—general truth)

1.3 In a series of related sentences, it is common to move from one established past time to another established past time by using another time expression.

Example:

We finished our work and then went to eat. After that, we went to a movie. It was late when we came home.

2. THE SIMPLE PRESENT TENSE AND TIME

2.1 General truths are usually expressed in the simple present tense.

Examples:

>   The administration sets the fees.
>   The planets revolve around the sun.
>   Water freezes at zero degrees Centigrade.
>   The moon circles around the Earth.

2.2 Customary or habitual action is usually expressed in the simple present tense. Time expressions often used with customary action: *annually, always, every day, usually, rarely, often, frequently, occasionally, sometimes, never, once in a while*, etc.

Examples:

>   I often go to town.
>   John rarely comes to see me.
>   He usually attends the meetings.
>   He frequently swims at four o'clock.
>   He jogs every morning.
>   She comes all the time.

2.3 Ability is usually expressed in the simple present tense.

Examples:

>   She swims very well.
>   I teach music.
>   Mary plays the piano, but John plays the trombone.
>   He jumps over three feet.

2.4 Perception or feelings of state or condition at the moment of speaking are usually expressed in the simple present tense: *see, hope, hear, smell, feel, seem, look, want, remember, forget, prefer, appear*

Examples:

>   He seems distressed.
>   I forget his name.
>   I want something to eat.
>   I remember the facts now.
>   The cheese smells bad.
>   The hamburger tastes delicious.

2.5 Future time (when certain verbs are used with future time expressions) may be expressed in the simple present tense. Some future time expressions are: *tomorrow, next week, next summer, Monday, Tuesday, in January, in February, at eight o'clock, before six o'clock,* etc.

Examples:

>   We leave tomorrow.
>   The train arrives at ten tonight.
>   James starts his trip next week.
>   Mary gets home in the morning.

3. THE SIMPLE PAST TENSE AND TIME

3.1 The simple past tense is used to write about situations that existed or occurred:

1. at a **definite** or **specific** time in the past (often indicated by time expressions such as *yesterday, last week, ten years ago,* etc.)

Examples:

> She went home an hour ago.
> I thought I recognized her.
> The baby cried during the performance.
> I received a package from home yesterday.
> Our team won the game.
> Mary played the piano while Jane sang.

Note: In the course of a paragraph or story, the past time may move from one definite past time to another definite past time.

Example:

> In my youth I lived in a small town. Later, we moved to the big city. After several years, my father bought a farm and we moved to a rural area.

3.2 The simple past tense may also be used to write about activities that existed or occurred:

1. over a **period of time** in the past, or

Examples:

> They played for several hours.
> He played rugby while he was in college.
> I waited for her all afternoon.
> During the semester break, the students went home.

2. at **intervals** in the past (**customary** or **habitual**).

Examples:

> She usually arrived late to the meetings last semester.
> He visited his mother from time to time.
> She walked to school every day when he was young.
> I heard the chimes regularly last year.

Another way of showing customary activity in the past is by using *used to.* (*Used to* has only a *past* and a *base* form.)

Examples:

> I used to go to school every day.
> Did you used to get there on time?

3.3 When writing about something which is **hypothetical, imaginary,** or **unreal,** it is common to use **past tense** even though the imagining is going on in the **present.** In this case, the aux-word *were* is used, even for singular subjects.

Examples:

> If I were the president, I would eliminate taxes; however, I am not, so I must pay them.
> If he should fall, he could break his neck.

Assignment 3:A

Write the passage below, supplying the correct present *or past* form of the verb or aux-word whose base form is beneath the blank.

FRESH BREAD

¹Whenever I _____ (smell) fresh bread baking, I _____ (think) of my youth and what fun it _____ (be) when I _____ (come) home from school and _____ (find) fresh loaves of bread on the table. ²Even now, if I _____ (close) my eyes, I _____ (seem) to taste the goodness of a thick slab of that bread lavishly spread with butter. ³Our family _____ (seem) to eat the bread as fast as mother _____ (can) make it. ⁴Twice a week she _____ (bake) a new batch. ⁵I always _____ (eat) all I _____ (can), yet I never _____ (tire) of that good bread my mother _____ (bake). ⁶Bread _____ (be) truly the "staff of life."

Assignment 3:B

Write the passage below, supplying the correct present *or past* form of the verb or aux-word whose base form is beneath the blank.

TASTE

¹Food frequently _____ (taste) different to different people. ²Several years ago, scientists _____ (test) different people with the same substance. ³To some it _____ (taste) bitter, while to others it _____ (have) no taste at all. ⁴Another substance _____ (taste) sweet to some people but _____ (seem) bitter to others. ⁵These experiments _____ (show) that there _____ (be) four different taste classes among people. ⁶There _____ (be) various "taste buds" located throughout the mouth. ⁷Taste _____ (depend) on these taste buds—little bumps located on the tongue, cheeks, and throat. ⁸Those on the tip of the tongue _____ (designate) sweetness. ⁹Those at the back _____ (catch) the bitter tastes. ¹⁰The cheeks _____ (pick) up sour tastes. ¹¹Flavor _____ (be) also a very important factor of taste. ¹²Flavor _____ (use) the eyes and nose in addition to the taste buds. ¹³In the past, I _____ (have) no excuse for not eating something I _____ (dislike). ¹⁴Now, when I don't like something, I _____ (blame) it on my taste buds and _____ (refuse) to eat it.

Verbs and Time 83

Assignment 3:C

Write the passage below, supplying the correct present *or past form of the verb or aux-word whose base form is beneath the blank.*

TOOLS AND PROGRESS

¹One of the qualities that _____ men superior to the beasts _____ their ability
                                    make   be
to make and use tools. ²Since early men's hands _____ not needed for moving around, they
                                                 be
_____ them to carry and use tools. ³The availability of their hands and their superior intelligence
  use
_____ civilization and progress possible for men.
  make

⁴Men's first tools _____ primitive by today's standards. ⁵A dead tree branch _____
                     be   become
a tool for knocking fruit down from a tree. ⁶Today, men _____ machines which _____
                                                          have   lift
them up into the trees to pick fruit easily and efficiently. ⁷On some farms, machines _____ fruit
                                                                                        harvest
and vegetables all by themselves. ⁸Men simply _____ these tools.
                                                guide

⁹Primitive men also _____ their tools as weapons. ¹⁰Many centuries ago, men
                      use
_____ heavy rocks to stout sticks and _____ clubs. ¹¹Attaching a sharpened
 attach   make
rock to the end of a long, thin stick _____ in a spear. ¹²Using these weapons _____
                                        result   allow
men to kill strong animals and each other.

¹³Modern men _____ more sophisticated tools as weapons. ¹⁴The invention of gunpowder
               use
_____ a new era in weaponry. ¹⁵Rifles and pistols _____ necessary tools for
  begin   become
both soldiers and hunters. ¹⁶Later men _____ more powerful explosives. ¹⁷Today, men
                                         develop
_____ the capacity to destroy themselves and the civilization which their hands and brains
  have
_____ centuries ago with the invention of simple tools. ¹⁸One only _____ that
  start   hope
modern man's intelligence _____ greater than the destructive powers that he, with his tools,
                            be
_____ .
 possess

4. THE *-ING* VERB FORM AND TIME

4.1 The timeless *-ing* verb form is used with the **present tense** aux-words *am, is,* and *are.* The use of the *-ing* form rather than the simple present tense emphasizes that the activity is **in progress** (not customary or habitual) and/or is **temporary** (not permanent). It may also indicate that the action is **repeated** many times.

4.2 **Activities in progress** expressed by the use of the aux + *-ing* verb form may take place at the moment of speaking/writing,

Examples:

>   Mary is watching television.
>   John is swimming in the pool.
>   The movie is playing now.
>   Mr. Jones is speaking.
>   She is listening to the concert.

or the activities in progress may **begin before** and **continue after** the moment of speaking/writing. They may **not** necessarily be taking place at the **exact** moment of speaking/writing.

Examples:

>   I am having a lot of trouble this semester.
>   The newspaper is presenting a series of John's articles.
>   He's doing biological research.
>   She is teaching a course in English at the college.
>   The office is collecting funds for the Red Cross.
>   They're having a lovely courtship.

4.3 **Future activities** may also be expressed by the use of the present tense aux-words *am*, *is*, and *are* plus the timeless *-ing* form of the verb when used with a **future time expression** such as *tomorrow, next year, this evening, tonight,* etc.

Examples:

>   We're going to Europe next summer.
>   I'm having Bill and Mary over on Sunday.
>   The boys on the team are giving a party this weekend.
>   We're leaving on our vacation next week.
>   I'm starting on a diet tomorrow.

4.4 The timeless *-ing* form of the verb is used with **past tense** aux-words *was* and *were* to show:

1. activities **in progress at a specific time in the past.** Time expressions indicating a specific past time are generally used.

Examples:

>   It was raining last night.
>   I was living in Syria at that time.
>   They were having a lot of trouble last semester.

2. activities **in progress when another event occurs.** These in-progress activities usually serve as a **background** for another activity which is expressed in the simple past tense.

Examples:

>   I thought about her while I was walking home.
>   The blowout occurred while we were passing another car.
>   He was steering the boat when the wave turned it over.

4.5 The use of the aux-word + *-ing* verb form combination emphasizes that the activity or condition is in progress, even though the condition or activity is normally considered habitual, customary, or a general truth.

Examples:

>   The sun rises every day.
>   Look! The sun is rising.

The sun sets in the west.
As the sun was slowly setting in the west, we finished the last chores of the day.
Henry jogs every morning.
Henry isn't jogging today because he's sick.

Note: The aux-word plus-*ing* verb form combinations are often called the present and past progressive tenses. Others call them the present and past continuous tenses.

Assignment 4:A

Write the passage below, supplying the correct -s, no-s, past, base, or past/present aux (am, is, are, was, were) +ing form of the verb or aux-word whose base form is shown beneath the blank.

RELAXING

¹Sometimes I just _____ to relax. ²I _____ my eyes and _____ my
　　　　　　　　　　like　　　　　　　close　　　　　　　　　let
thoughts come and go. ³Sometimes someone _____ me and _____ me what I
　　　　　　　　　　　　　　　　　　　　disturb　　　　　　　　ask
_____ or what I _____ of. ⁴Usually I _____ that I _____
　do　　　　　　think　　　　　　　　reply　　　　　　meditate
because that _____ much busier than saying that I _____. ⁵Then people usually
　　　　　sound　　　　　　　　　　　　　　　　rest
_____ me alone although sometimes they _____ and _____.
leave　　　　　　　　　　　　　　　　　stop　　　　　　talk
⁶Teachers and mothers simply do not _____. ⁷They _____ all the time and
　　　　　　　　　　　　　　　understand　　　　work
_____ others need to _____ too. ⁸They _____ not very tolerant
think　　　　　　　work　　　　　　　　be
of laziness. ⁹Just last week, while I _____ on a chair, my mother quickly _____ a
　　　　　　　　　　　　　　　sit　　　　　　　　　　　　　　　find
task to keep me busy because she _____ that I _____ nothing. ¹⁰While I
　　　　　　　　　　　　　　　see　　　　　　do
_____ I _____ that the next time I _____ it would _____
work　　　decide　　　　　　　　　　rest　　　　　　　be
somewhere out of my mother's sight.

Assignment 4:B

Write the passage below, supplying the correct -s, no-s, past, base, or past/present aux (am, is, are, was, were) + -ing form of the verb or aux-word whose base form is shown beneath the blank.

COSMIC COLLISIONS

¹You may _____ that the earth beneath your feet _____ stable, but in reality it
　　　　think　　　　　　　　　　　　　　　　be
_____ not. ²It _____ to be stationary, of course, but right now the earth
　be　　　　　seem
_____ through space at a tremendous speed, 66,600 miles per hour! ³It _____
move　　　　　　　　　　　　　　　　　　　　　　　　　　　　　revolve
on its axis also. ⁴Do you _____ that at this very moment you _____ around in
　　　　　　　　realize　　　　　　　　　　　　　　go
circles at close to one thousand miles per hour?

86 SENTENCE CONSTRUCTION

⁵Most people _____ no idea of the speed at which they _____ through the
       have   travel
universe. ⁶What they don't _____ doesn't _____ them. ⁷They _____
                            know   frighten   be
unaware that other objects, besides the planet earth, _____ through space at fantastic speeds also.
                                                       hurtle
⁸Nothing _____ these comets, meteors, planets, and stars from colliding with each other. ⁹The
          prevent
only thing that _____ such collisions infrequent _____ the immensity of space.
                 make   be
¹⁰The chances _____ small that one heavenly body will _____ into another one.
               be   crash
¹¹The results when they do, however, _____ disastrous. ¹²A meteorite once _____
                                      be   hit
the earth in northern Arizona. ¹³It _____ a crater over 4,000 feet wide and nearly 600 feet deep.
                                     make
¹⁴In 1908 a large meteorite _____ into the earth in central Siberia. ¹⁵The resultant explosion
                             crash
_____ windows fifty miles away, _____ over eighty million trees, and
 break   burn
_____ 1,500 reindeer.
 kill

¹⁶People's ignorance of impending danger, although comforting, will not _____ them from
                                                                         save
disaster. ¹⁷Knowing that a disaster _____ however, _____ not much protection
                                     approach   be
either.

Assignment 4:C

Write the passage below, supplying the correct -s, no-s, past, base, or past/present aux (am, is, are, was, were) + -ing form of the verb or aux-word whose base form is shown beneath the blank.

A PARTY

¹Last night when I _____ them, the Browns _____ a party. ²They _____
                    call   plan   go
over the guest list and _____ about what type of entertainment to _____ and what
                         argue   have
refreshments to _____. ³They _____ and _____ each other's
                 serve   consider   reject
suggestions for a bridge party, a movie, or simple parlor games.

⁴When I _____ them this morning, they still _____ about it. ⁵They
         see   talk
_____ their party to _____ different. ⁶I _____ that they might
 want   be   suggest
_____ a treasure hunt. ⁷They _____ that _____ a good idea, and
 have   think   be
now they _____ the refreshments. ⁸I hope they can _____ on what to
          plan   agree
_____ and where to _____ the treasure.
 eat   hide

5. THE EARLIER-THAN-ESTABLISHED-TIME RELATIONSHIP

5.1 Once a present or past time has been established (by either a time expression or a verb form), related times—earlier and later—are indicated by certain aux-word and timeless verb form combinations.

The aux-words *have/has* are always followed by the timeless *d-t-n* form of a verb. This combination is used to show a time **earlier than the established present time**.

The aux-word *had* followed by the *d-t-n* form is used to show a time earlier than the established past time.

5.2 This **earlier-than-the-present-time** relationship includes:

1. activities that have existed or occurred sometime before the time of speaking/writing. The exact time is not always indicated.

    Some common time expressions which indicate an action before the present time are *since, yet, already, ever,* and *for a long time*. Frequency words such as *several times, often, at last,* etc., may indicate one or more times.

Examples:

   I have read that book several times.
   She has written three essays already.
   She has been at the university since last September.
   I have been here far too long.

   The time expression *just* is often used to indicate or emphasize a very recent earlier time.

Examples:

   We have just arrived.
   I have just returned from a trip to the Orient.

2. activities which began in the past, have continued up to the present time, and will probably extend beyond this time.

Examples:

   I have listened to the choir broadcast for years.
   We have known these students for a long time.
   I have always liked that girl.
   Susan has been in Greece since she left here.

5.3 The **earlier-than-the-past-time** relationship includes activities that occurred or existed before another activity in the past.

Examples:

   I had just finished my assignment when Bill arrived.
   I had already finished my homework when he invited me to go for a ride.
   They had done their work before the bell rang.
   I had never heard that story before I attended the lecture.
   She had studied English before she entered college.

5.4 An earlier time reference may even become a new established time.

Example:

   Our plane left on July 12. We *had packed* our bags many days before. We didn't pack many things that we wanted to take because they didn't fit.

Assignment 5:A

Write the passage below, supplying the correct -s, no-s, past, base, or have/has or had + d-t-n form of the verb or aux-word whose base form is beneath the blank.

NOAH'S ARK? I*

¹Most people in the world today _____ the story of Noah's Ark. ²Relatively few of them
                                        hear
_____, however, that for many years there _____ reports that a large structure
    know   be
that _____ like a boat _____ buried beneath ice and snow at the 14,000 foot level
        look   lie
on Mount Ararat in Eastern Turkey. ³The structure _____ as large as modern battleships, but
                                                          be
it _____ made of wood. ⁴When they _____ these reports, many people
     be   hear
_____ that Noah's Ark _____ found.
   believe   be

⁵Since 700 B.C., historians and explorers _____ such a structure on Mt. Ararat. ⁶In 1840,
                                                  mention
a Turkish expedition which _____ checking for damage caused by an earthquake which
                                    be
_____ earlier that year, _____ a gigantic wooden ship on Mt. Ararat. ⁷Some
   occur   discover
men even _____ plans to _____ the structure and _____ it at the
              make   excavate   exhibit
1893 World's Fair in Chicago.

⁸In 1970, an old man named George Hagopian _____ that 68 years earlier, in 1902, he
                                                    claim
_____ the Ark. ⁹He _____ that his uncle _____ him up and he
   visit   report   lift
_____ on the roof of the Ark.
   walk

*(Information for these three passages has been taken from *In Search of Noah's Ark* by Dave Balsiger and Charles E. Sellier, Jr.)

Assignment 5:B

Write the passage below, supplying the correct -s, no-s, past, base, or have/has or had + d-t-n form of the verb or aux-word whose base form is beneath the blank.

NOAH'S ARK? II

¹Since the turn of the century other expeditions _____ the difficut journey up Mt. Ararat also.
                                                         make
²They _____ Mt. Ararat to _____ treacherous. ³Storms and blizzards
        find   be
_____ on the mountain nearly every day. ⁴Avalanches _____ many climbers.
   occur   kill
⁵In the past few decades, several earthquakes _____ in Eastern Turkey. ⁶Some Ark
                                                      occur
experts _____ that these earthquakes _____ the wooden structure into several
          report   break
pieces. ⁷Some of these pieces _____ from their original position to other locations farther down
                                      slip
the mountain where they _____ more accessible.
                                be

⁸By late 1955, a French explorer named Fernand Navarra _____ wood from the structure.
                                                          recover
⁹Modern dating tests conducted since then _____ that the wood _____ thousands
                                          reveal   be
of years old.

¹⁰Some modern critics _____ fault with the reports of people who _____ the
                      find   visit
site where the structure _____ located. ¹¹However, they cannot _____ that
                         be   deny
since 1856 over two hundred people on twenty-three different occasions _____ seeing the
                                                                        report
structure on Mt. Ararat.

Assignment 5:C

Write the passage below, supplying the correct -s, *no-*s, *past, base, or* have/has *or* had + d-t-n *form of the verb or aux-word whose base form is beneath the blank.*

NOAH'S ARK? III

¹Today, exploration of Mount Ararat _____ not allowed. ²In 1974, Turkish government
                                     be
officials _____ regulations prohibiting foreigners from traveling to Mt. Ararat. ³Since then,
          announce
they _____ a number of reasons for these regulations.
     give

⁴They _____ that the Russians _____ a military missile facility only forty
      explain   build
miles from the mountain across the Turkish-Soviet border. ⁵This development _____ Mt. Ararat
                                                                             cause
to be classified as a restricted military zone.

⁶Although travel to Mt. Ararat _____ prohibited, for the past few years many adventurers
                                be
_____ to _____ plans to _____ the mountain when the ban is
continue   make   visit
lifted. ⁷One explorer named McCollum _____ his plan to use a large helicopter to
                                      announce
_____ supplies and equipment to the site. ⁸He _____ to _____ the
airlift   promise   donate
helicopter to the Turkish government once the expedition _____ its purpose, but his plan
                                                          accomplish
_____ to receive Turkish approval. ⁹Since he originally _____ the expedition in
fail   plan
1970, McCollum _____ his large helicopter, but he _____ still ready, for he
               sell   be
_____ it with another helicopter which _____ even more horsepower. ¹⁰He
replace   have
still _____ to prove beyond doubt that the structure on Mt. Ararat _____ really
      hope   be
Noah's Ark.

6. THE LATER-THAN-ESTABLISHED-TIME RELATIONSHIP

6.1 The **later-than-the-present-established-time** relationship is expressed by using the aux-word *will* (or *shall*) or the phrase *am/is/are going to* plus the base form of the verb.

Examples:

We *hope* they *will leave* soon.
(established present) (later time)

I *can't do* it now, but I *will do* it later.
(established present) (later time)

He *will fail* if he *doesn't study*.
(later time) (present time)

He *is going to leave* tomorrow.
  (later time)

I *am going to do* my homework in a few minutes.
  (later time)

6.2 The **later-than-the-past-established-time** relationship is shown by using the aux-word *would* or the phrase *was/were going to* plus the base form of the verb.

Examples:

He *promised* he *would help* us tomorrow.
(established past) (later time) (later time)

Yesterday, he *said* he *was going to do* it.
(established past) (later time)

They *told* us they *were going to visit* Hawaii next summer.
(established past) (later time) (later time)

The later time in the past can extend beyond the present into the future.

Example:

Five years ago he *predicted* that the world *would end* in 1999.
  (established past) (later time)

6.3 A later time reference may become a new established time.

Example:

Joe *said* he *would call* me after the game, and he *didn't forget*.

(est. past) *(later time)* *(new established time)*

Assignment 6:A

Write the passage below, supplying the correct -s, no-s, past, base, have/has *or* had + d-t-n *form,* will, would + *base form, or* is/am/are, was/were going to + *base form of the verb or aux-word whose base form is beneath the blank.*

FALSE PROPHETS

[1]Last week I _____ a man. [2]He _____ a sign that _____ that the
              see   carry   say

world _____ the next day. [3]I _____ him if he really _____ the
        end   ask   think

world _____ to an end so soon. [4]He _____ that he _____ , but
        come   reply   do

Verbs and Time   91

nothing _____(happen)_____ the next day.

⁵Yesterday, I _____(encounter)_____ him again. ⁶He _____(carry)_____ the same sign. ⁷It _____(say)_____ that the world _____(end)_____ today. ⁸I _____(ask)_____ him why it _____(fail)_____ to end last week, but he _____(do)_____ not answer me.

⁹The world _____(be)_____ full of people who _____(make)_____ false predictions. ¹⁰It _____(be)_____ not difficult to _____(find)_____ someone who _____(believe)_____ that there soon _____(be)_____ a great earthquake in California and that the west coast of the United States _____(slip)_____ into the ocean.

¹¹Several years ago, some people _____(predict)_____ an earthquake in my hometown. ¹²They even _____(specify)_____ the day and the hour it _____(occur)_____. ¹³That day and hour _____(come)_____ and _____(go)_____, but nothing disastrous _____(happen)_____. ¹⁴Nearly a year later there _____(be)_____ a minor earthquake. ¹⁵The same people _____(be)_____ very quick to _____(announce)_____ that they _____(predict)_____ it _____(happen)_____, but everybody just laughed. ¹⁶It _____(take)_____ no special talent to _____(predict)_____ an event after it _____(happen)_____.

Assignment 6:B

Write the passage below, supplying the correct -s, no-s, past, base, have/has or had + d-t-n form, will, would + base form, or is/am/are, was/were going to + base form of the verb or aux-word whose base form is beneath the blank.

AN ASTRONAUT

¹I once _____(think)_____ I _____(like)_____ to _____(be)_____ an astronaut. ²Whenever I _____(feel)_____ overworked or hemmed in, I _____(dream)_____ of leaving everything and getting away from it all. ³I _____(imagine)_____ how great it _____(be)_____ to _____(soar)_____ weightlessly through space. ⁴I _____(think)_____ there _____(be)_____ nothing to _____(do)_____ but relax and enjoy myself. ⁵However, when I _____(see)_____ a space capsule for the first time, I _____(change)_____ my mind. ⁶Now I no longer _____(want)_____ to _____(become)_____ an astronaut, as astronauts _____(have)_____ more to _____(do)_____ than I _____(have)_____. ⁷When an astronaut _____(go)_____ into orbit, I _____(know)_____ he _____(get)_____ less sleep than I _____(do)_____

92 SENTENCE CONSTRUCTION

now. ⁸He _____(have)_____ to _____(be)_____ alert. ⁹Quarters _____(be)_____ crowded. ¹⁰It _____(take)_____ more effort to _____(do)_____ things in the capsule. ¹¹Without gravity, nothing _____(stay)_____ put. ¹²He _____(have)_____ to _____(hang)_____ on or _____(be)_____ strapped down to _____(stay)_____ in one place. ¹³Although previously I _____(think)_____ it _____(be)_____ fun to leave the earth, now I _____(know)_____ I _____(have)_____ to _____(think)_____ of some new way to _____(get)_____ away from it all.

Assignment 6:C

Write the passage below, supplying the correct -s, no-s, past, base, have/has or had + d-t-n form, will, would + base form, or is/am/are, was/were going to + base form of the verb or aux-word whose base form is beneath the blank.

DOOMSDAY!

¹Many people _____(think)_____ that men _____(destroy)_____ themselves eventually. ²Some _____(forecast)_____ atomic wars which _____(devastate)_____ this planet. ³Others _____(predict)_____ that society's pollution _____(destroy)_____ modern civilization. ⁴According to these people, smog, oil spills, the leakage of stored chemicals, and the like _____(be)_____ man's doom. ⁵Some _____(feel)_____ that the moral breakdown of society _____(reduce)_____ man to an animal state. ⁶Others _____(point)_____ to the increasing frequency and severity of natural disasters—earthquakes, hurricanes, winter storms, tidal waves, etc.—and _____(say)_____ that nature _____(overthrow)_____ man's fragile civilization.

⁷Predictors of destruction _____(be)_____ not new, of course. ⁸Almost as soon as civilization _____(start)_____ people _____(begin)_____ to _____(predict)_____ that it _____(end)_____. ⁹No one really _____(know)_____ how or when the world _____(end)_____. ¹⁰When we _____(find)_____ out, it _____(be)_____ too late.

7. SUMMARY OF TIME AND TENSE RELATIONSHIPS

The diagrams below illustrate the different time relationships with their corresponding verb forms which have been discussed in the two previous chapters (6 and 7).

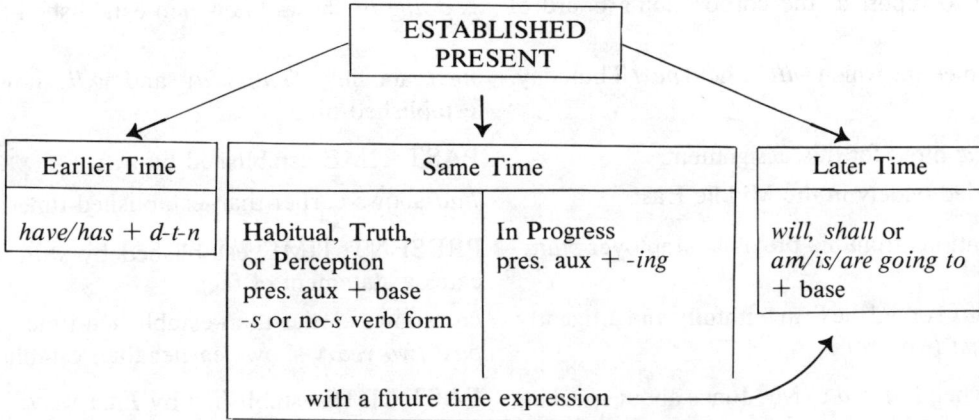

Example:

    I am lost in the desert. I am crawling across the sand. I see mirages everywhere. I have not had a drink of water for two days. I think I am going to die. I hope someone will rescue me.

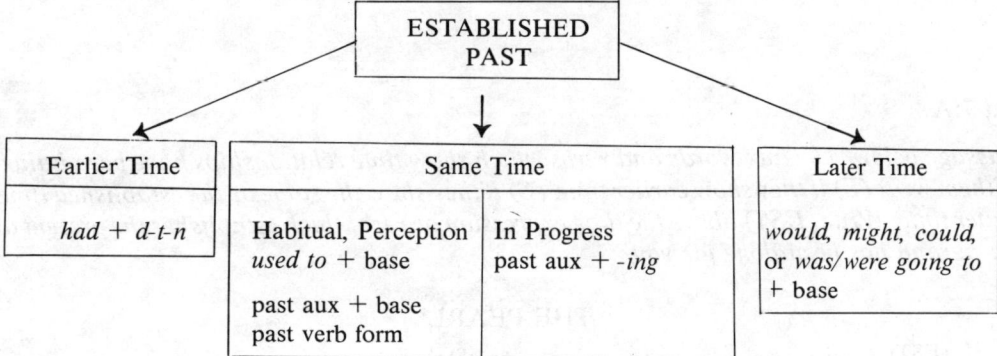

Example:

    Last month, I was lost in the desert. I was crawling across the sand. I saw mirages everywhere. I had not had a drink of water for two days. I thought I was going to die. I hoped someone would rescue me, and somebody did.

94 SENTENCE CONSTRUCTION

Now, referring to the previous diagrams, study the following examples:

John Jones *works* for an international corporation.	PRESENT TIME established by *works*
He *has recently* returned from a business trip to Japan.	*has* and *recently* show earlier-than-established-time
He *is going* to report to the corporation's board of directors.	*is going to* shows later-than-established-time
at their *next* meeting which *will* be held *next* Thursday.	*next* and *next Thursday* and *will* show later-than-established-time
Before he *was* hired for this assignment,	PAST TIME established by *was*
he *had* traveled widely in the Middle East.	*had* shows earlier-than-established-time
Recommendations from his previous employer *state*,	PRESENT TIME established by *state* which indicates a statement of fact
"Mr. Jones *has* served the firm faithfully and diligently during the *past two years*."	*has* shows earlier-than-established-time *past two years* shows earlier-than-established-time
Last week, when I *talked* to Mr. Jones about speaking to our business students,	PAST TIME established by *Last week*; *talked* shows same established time
he *said*	*said* shows same as established time
he *would* be happy to	*would* shows later-than-established-time
explain the challenges of intercultural business to us.	

Assignment 7:A

Copy the passage below. The aux-words and verbs which show time relationships have been italicized. Above each one of them write (E) if they show earlier time, (S) if they show the same as the established time, and (L) if they show later time. Write (EST) above the time expression or verb which establishes the present or past time. The first paragraph has been done for you.

THE PEARL*

(EST)   (S)
In the town they *tell* the story of the great pearl. . . . They *tell* of Kino the fisherman, and of his wife, Juana, and
                                       (E)   (E)
of the baby Coyotito. And because the story *has been told* so often, it *has taken* root in every man's mind.
                                              ****

¹Kino *awakened* in the near dark. ²The stars still *shone* and the day *had drawn* only a pale wash of light in the lower sky to the east. ³The roosters *had been crowing* for some time, and the early pigs *were* already *beginning* their ceaseless turning of twigs and bits of wood to see whether anything to eat *had been overlooked*. ⁴Outside the brush house in the tuna clump, a covey of little birds *chittered* and *flurried* with their wings.
    ⁵Kino *heard* the little splash of morning waves on the beach. ⁶It *was* very good. ⁷Kino *closed* his eyes again to listen to his music. ⁸Perhaps he alone *did* this and perhaps all of his people *did* it. ⁹His people *had* once *been* great makers of songs so that everything they *saw* or *thought* or *did* or *heard became* a song.
    ¹⁰The dawn *came* quickly now, a wash, a glow, a lightness, and then an explosion of fire as the sun *arose* out of the Gulf. ¹¹Kino *looked* down to cover his eyes from the glare. ¹²He *could hear* the pat of the corncakes in the house and the rich smell of them on the cooking plate. ¹³The ants *were* busy on the ground, big black ones with shiny bodies, and little dusty quick ants. ¹⁴Kino *watched* with the detachment of God while a dusty ant frantically *tried* to escape the sand trap an ant lion *had dug* for him.

*John Steinbeck, *The Pearl* (New York: Viking, 1947). Used by permission.

Assignment 7:B

Copy the passage below. The aux-words and verbs which show time relationships have been italicized. Above each one of them write (E) if they show earlier time, (S) if they show the same as the established time, and (L) if they show later time. Write (EST) above the time expression or verb which establishes the present or past time.

FIRE I*

¹Actually, although Bart *hated* all fires desperately, he *realized* that this one *had* not *done* any great damage. ²It *had wiped out* the underbrush and small trees, but the underbrush *would spring up* fast and very few of the small trees *would* ever *have grown* to maturity anyway, against the competition of the big ones. ³Of the big trees very few *had been killed,* because the fire *had* mostly *stayed* close to the ground. ⁴The chief damage *would be* that the fire, eating at the bases of the large trees, *had burned* through the bark in places, and *caused* what the lumbermen called "cat-faces." ⁵Boring insects *would work* into these cat-faces, and in a few years there *would be* a lot of sick and dying trees. ⁶Bart *put* the map into his pocket, and *started* to slide down the steep trail where he *had set* the first back-fire. ⁷Soon, having to pick his way with the aid of the flashlight, he *was working* along the undercut line that the jumpers *had built.* ⁸An occasional blackened cone lying in the ditch *showed* that it *had* not *been* labor wasted.

*George R. Stewart, *Fire* (New York: Random House, 1948), pp. 141–142. Used by permission.

Assignment 7:C

Copy the passage below. The aux-words and verbs which show time relationships have been italicized. Above each of them write (E) if they show earlier time, (S) if they show the same as the established time, and (L) if they show later time. Write (EST) above the time expression or verb which establishes the present or past time.

FIRE II*

¹Everywhere the small trees *had been wiped out,* as if a plague *had swept* through a nation, sparing some adults but killing all the babies and children. ²In the next few years the still-standing older trees *might reseed* the ground beneath them, but once they *had been logged off* or *fallen* from disease or mere old age, only tiny saplings *would remain*—not vigorous young trees reaching up fifty or a hundred feet already.

³But that *would be* the best that *could be expected.* ⁴Where the crown-fires *had raged,* no trees *were left* to spread seed, and brush *would spring up* faster than forest. ⁵Once established, it *would remain* for many years, perhaps for centuries, yielding only foot by foot as the forest *pressed* in around the edges. ⁶Indeed, some *said* pessimistically that the forests of California *had established* themselves in some wetter cycle of centuries and that the brush, once rooted, *would remain* until some wetter cycle *returned.*

⁷The flaming disaster of those few days *would* not *be undone* in a hundred years. ⁸Even after five hundred, a skilled forester *might* still *be* able to trace the scar of that old burn.

*George R. Stewart, *Fire* (New York: Random House, 1948), pp. 319–320. Used by permission.

8. LATER OR EARLIER TIME WITH -*ING* FORMS

Later and earlier relationships of activities in progress can be shown by a combination of the normal earlier (*has/have; had*) or later (*will, would; am/is/are going to, was/were going to*) aux-words plus *been* or *be* followed by an *-ing* verb form.

Examples:

        I *have been reading* this book for hours.
  (earlier-than-present time in progress)

        I *will be going* home soon.
  (later-than-present time in progress)

    Before I helped him yesterday, John *had been trying* to fix the car for hours.
          (earlier-than-past time in progress)

He said he *would have been working* on it forever if someone hadn't helped him.
    (later-than-past time in progress)

Paragraph example:
I saw Jennifer at the corner yesterday. She was waiting for Mike. She *had been waiting* for nearly an hour. She said she *was going to wait* another five minutes. Then she *would be leaving*.

Assignment 8:A

Add aux-words and/or verbs (and any other words you wish) that agree with the subjects and time expressions below. Write your complete sentence in paragraph form. (Be sure that your sentences are connected to a central theme.

MY FATHER

1. One day last week, my father

2. Previously, he

3. So he thought he

4. Sometimes my father

5. Up until now, my mother

6. However, right now she

7. Someday she

8. At the present time, the family

9. In the future, some family members

10. Eventually, we

Assignment 8:B

Add aux-words and/or verbs (and any other words you wish) that agree with the subjects and time expressions below. Write your complete sentences in paragraph form. (Be sure that your sentences are connected to a central theme.)

MY CLASS

1. Often, my classmates

2. Frequently, the teacher

3. Though sometimes, he

4. In the past, the students

5. Up until now they

6. In the future, they

7. Nearly always, the classroom

8. The textbooks never

9. Next year, things

10. Then the class

98   SENTENCE CONSTRUCTION

Assignment 8:C

Add aux-words and/or verbs (and any other words you wish) that agree with the subjects and time expressions below. Write your complete sentences in paragraph form. (Be sure that your sentences are connected to a central theme.)

AN ASSEMBLY

1. For years, an assembly

2. Frequently this assembly

3. However, in the past

4. Last year, it

5. After that, the show

6. Up until last week, it

7. Before that the music

8. At present the main concerns

9. In the future, the participants

10. Then the assemblies

9. MODAL + *HAVE* COMBINATIONS

Sometimes the timeless aux-word *have* (followed by the *d-t-n* form of a verb) comes after a modal. This combination *cannot* be used for all meanings of the modals (see Chapter 4, Section 8).

For example, the modal *must* has two meanings:

1. obligation   You must do your homework.   (It is a requirement.)
2. probability   You must be smart.   (You are learning very quickly.)

When *must* is used to show obligation, it *cannot* be followed by *have* + *d-t-n*.

Adding *have* changes the meaning of obligation to probability.

You must have done your homework.   (You got a good grade.)

The listing below shows which modals can be followed by *have* + *d-t-n* and which meanings are changed.

An asterisk (*) indicates that adding *have* changes the meaning.

A double asterisk (**) indicates that *have* cannot be added because the resulting combination is not semantically appropriate.

	without *have*	with *have*
CAN		
ability	Bill can swim.	**
inability	John can't do it.	John can't have done it.
possibility	It can get cold here at times.	**
request	Can you help me?	**
COULD		
ability	Joan could write well.	* (to possibility/probability)
possibility/probability	We could eat at a restaurant.	We could have eaten at a restaurant.
request	He asked me if I could go with him.	* (to possibility/probability)
MAY		
possibility	He may be the man you're after.	He may have been the man you're after.
permission	May I go now?	**
MIGHT		
possibility	John might get the job.	John might have gotten the job.
MUST		
obligation	You must work hard to get ahead.	* (to probability)
probability	She must be your girlfriend.	She must have been your girlfriend.
SHOULD		
obligation/advisability	He should pay his taxes.	He should have paid his taxes.
probability	The oranges should be ripe by now.	The oranges should have been ripe by now.
WILL		
request	Will you do it?	**
later time	He will finish by tomorrow.	He will have finished by tomorrow.
WOULD		
request	Would you come with me?	* (to possibility)
habitual past	When we were young we would often miss school.	* (to possibility)
condition/possibility/probability	If I had their address, I would write them a letter.	If I had had their address, I would have written them a letter.

Assignment 9:A

Write the passage below, supplying appropriate aux-word and verb form combinations. Use the modal + have + d-t-n combination when it is called for.

A STRANGE SIGHT

[1] When I saw Mr. Finstrom the other day, he was in a funny position. [2] His head and shoulders were inside his house, but his feet were sticking out the window.

[3] I didn't know what _____ (happen), but I used my imagination and came up with several possibilities. [4] He _____ (sneak) out of the house and avoiding the front door. [5] On the other hand, he _____ (enter) the house through the window because he _____ (forgotten) or lost his house key. [6] There were some other, more imaginative possibilities as well. [7] Perhaps some gangsters _____ (take) his family hostage and they _____ (hold) them in the living room. [8] In that case, Mr. Finstrom _____ (escape) through the window on his way to get help. [9] He and his wife _____ (have) an argument. [10] If so, she _____ (nail) the door shut to keep him out.

[11] As it turned out, the answer was not nearly that unusual. [12] Mr. Finstrom _____ (hire) some people to paint the inside of his house. [13] As professional painters, they _____ (know) better, but they _____ (not think) when they painted the inside of the door frames. [14] They _____ (finish) and _____ (leave) the house earlier in the day. [15] By the time Mr. Finstrom got home, the paint _____ (dry) and the doors were stuck. [16] The doors _____ (not open) because of the glue-like paint. [17] Crawling through the window was the only way he _____ (get) into the house.

Assignment 9:B

Write the passage below, supplying appropriate aux-word and verb form combinations. Use the modal + have + d-t-n combination when it is called for.

A TRAFFIC ACCIDENT

[1] There was an automobile accident near school early this morning. [2] Like all accidents, it _____ (not happen), but it did. [3] The driver of one car had a hard time believing that the accident _____ (happen) at all. [4] He kept walking around with his hands on his head repeating, "This _____ (not happen) to me. [5] Things like this happen to other people, but *not* to me." [6] The driver of the other car assured him that, without a doubt, it really _____ (happen). [7] The investigating policeman kept asking what _____ (happen), but he couldn't get a straight story.

⁸The first driver admitted that he _____(pay)_____ more attention to driving but that he _____(think)_____ of something else. ⁹He couldn't remember what it was that he _____(think)_____ about.

¹⁰My first impression was that the second driver _____(be)_____ drunk. ¹¹He shouted and got red as if he _____(drink)_____, but later I decided that he _____(be)_____ upset and not drunk. ¹²He insisted that the accident was not his fault, but the policeman seemed to think that he _____(avoid)_____ the other car if he _____(drive)_____ defensively. ¹³Obviously, he _____(not look out)_____ for the other guy like he _____(be)_____, but I couldn't see how the accident _____(be)_____ his fault. ¹⁴At any rate, I'm not the judge.

¹⁵Perhaps by now, the policeman _____(figure out)_____ exactly what happened and who was at fault. ¹⁶By tomorrow, the accident _____(become)_____ just one more traffic statistic.

Assignment 9:C

Write the passage below, supplying appropriate aux-word and verb form combinations. Use the modal + have + d-t-n combination when it is called for.

A MURDER MYSTERY

¹The murder was a terrible thing, but it seemed even worse because no one had any idea who _____(commit)_____ it. ²It _____(be)_____ the butler. ³Butlers are always prime suspects, but he had a good alibi. ⁴The victim's wife _____(be)_____ accused, but there were witnesses who _____(be)_____ with her at the time of the crime. ⁵Therefore, it was concluded that she _____(be not)_____ guilty. ⁶The detectives thought that the murder _____(commit)_____ by a suspicious neighbor, but they had no proof.

⁷The cause of death was even more elusive. ⁸There was no doubt that the victim was dead, but there were no indications of what _____(cause)_____ him to die. ⁹There were no marks on the body, but poison _____(use)_____ by the murderer. ¹⁰That possibility could not be ruled out until after an autopsy _____(perform)_____ by the coroner. ¹¹By then the guilty party _____(escape)_____.

¹²The detectives couldn't wait that long. ¹³They investigated further and found a clue they _____(overlook)_____ before. ¹⁴If they _____(give up)_____, they never _____(find)_____ it. ¹⁵This clue led to others until the mystery _____(solve)_____. ¹⁶The murderer _____(get)_____ away if it hadn't been for that one, small clue and the persistence of the detectives.

7
THE SENTENCE

1. SUBJECT AND PREDICATE

In order to write a sentence, you need two things:

1. something to write about, and
2. something to say about it.

These are usually called (1) the **subject** and (2) the **predicate**.

Each of these can be the length you choose: from very short (one word each) to very long.

Examples:

one word each:

Sue / won.

very long:

The maximum price for a primary fish shipper sale of fresh fish or sea-food (except shrimp, salmon or halibut) to a retailer or purveyor of meals where the sale is negotiated or made at a branch warehouse as herein defined and where the fish or sea-food is sold and delivered from the stock of a primary fish shipper wholesaler's branch warehouse which is remote from his main place of doing business, and at which warehouse the primary fish shipper employs two or more full-time employees who are stationed at and engaged in making sales and performing services solely for the primary fish shipper from such warehouse / is the price listed in Table D in 22 plus the allowance provided in 6 for a service and delivery sale where such sale is made, plus the transportation allowance in 9 plus the appropriate container allowance in 21.

(It is not recommended that you write sentences like this "monster," which came from a government wholesale fish sales manual.)

Assignment 1:A

Supply subjects for the following predicates. Write your complete sentences in paragraph form. You have a wide choice of subjects, but be sure the subjects you choose make sense when used with the predicates. Also, make sure the subjects relate to each other. This is a story!

A BASEBALL GAME

1. _____ liked to attend baseball games.

2. _____ usually went right after payday.

3. _____ enjoyed seeing the home team play baseball.

4. _____ cheered and booed with the crowd.

5. _____ usually didn't cost more than five dollars each.

6. _____ would spend more than that.

7. _____ were sold during the game.

8. _____ bought a hat to shade her face from the sun.

9. _____ got a souvenir pennant to decorate his room.

10. _____ wanted something to eat.

11. _____ usually went home tired and happy, but broke.

12. _____ looked forward to the next trip to the ball park.

Assignment 1:B

Supply subjects for the following predicates. Write your complete sentences in paragraph form. You have a wide choice of subjects, but be sure the subjects you choose make sense when used with the predicates. Also, make sure the subjects relate to each other. This is a story!

THE TEST

1. _____ failed the test last week.

2. _____ couldn't have been worse.

3. _____ seemed hard at the time.

4. _____ wasn't really that difficult.

5. _____ could have passed without any problems.

6. _____ stayed up too late the night before.

7. _____ didn't do the homework.

8. _____ explained it to the class.

9. _____ didn't listen carefully.

10. _____ should have paid more atatention.

11. _____ warned the students about their study habits.

12. _____ shouldn't have talked so much.

13. _____ should have known better.

104 SENTENCE CONSTRUCTION

14. _____ learned a good lesson.

15. _____ will do things differently next time.

Assignment 1:C

Supply subjects for the following predicates. Write your complete sentences in paragraph form. You have a wide choice of subjects, but be sure the subjects you choose make sense when used with the predicates. Also, make sure the subjects relate to each other. This is a story!

A DECISION

1. _____ wanted to attend college.

2. _____ said it was a good idea.

3. _____ stood in his way, however.

4. _____ was one of them.

5. _____ was another.

6. _____ was a third problem.

7. _____ was able to overcome all these difficulties.

8. _____ had to be made as to which college to attend.

9. _____ were very far from home.

10. _____ was too high.

11. _____ finally made a decision and went to college.

2. SIMPLE AND COMPLEX SENTENCES

2.1 A simple sentence has one subject and one predicate.

Correct simple sentences are fundamental to acceptable writing. They can be combined in a variety of ways to make longer, complex sentences.

Example:

Simple sentences:
    Trees are one of nature's most versatile creations.
    Trees vary in size.
    Trees vary in density.
    Trees grow under many different circumstances.
    Trees grow at many different rates.

Combined:
    Growing under many different circumstances and at many different rates, trees, one of nature's most versatile creations, vary in age, size, and density.

2.2 A complex sentence can be broken down into simple sentences. (This skill may be useful in increasing reading comprehension.

Example:

Combined:

Walking to class this morning, George, my friend, stumbled, dropped his books, and lost his math homework which he had worked on all night.

Simple sentences:

George walked to class this morning.
George is my friend.
George stumbled.
George dropped his books.
George lost his math homework.
George worked on his math homework all night.

In this book you will learn to write correct, simple sentences.

In Book II (*Sentence Combination*), you will learn a number of ways to combine the simple sentences you have learned to write in this book.

3. SHIFTERS

3.1 **Shifters*** are words or groups of words that occur at the beginning or end of a sentence but are not part of the basic sentence. They provide extra information about the basic sentence such as **time, reason, condition,** or **contrast**.

They are called shifters because they can be moved from the front position to the end position, or vice versa, without a change in meaning.

Examples:

Before the race, John exercised daily. (time)
John exercised daily before the race.

Because they were afraid of failing, the students didn't even try. (reason)
The students didn't even try because they were afraid of failing.

If it rains, there will be no ball game. (condition)
There will be no ball game if it rains.

Even though he had problems, John kept on trying. (contrast)
John kept on trying even though he had problems.

3.2 To make a yes/no question from a statement that has a front shifter, move the shifter to the end position before moving the aux-word in front of the subject.

Examples:

Last summer George couldn't find a job.
George couldn't find a job last summer.
Couldn't George find a job last summer?

Because she didn't study, Mary failed the test.
Mary failed the test because she didn't study.
Did Mary fail the test because she didn't study?

3.3 Generally front shifters are separated from the basic sentence by commas. However, with many short (less than four words) shifters no comma is needed. When the shifter appears at the end commas are seldom used. (Shifters are discussed in more detail in Chapter 11.)

*Robert L. Allen's term.

106 SENTENCE CONSTRUCTION

Assignment 3:A

Make yes/no questions from the following sentences. Be sure to move the shifters from the front to the end of each sentence before moving the aux-words.

A DECISION

1. For a high school graduate, deciding whether to continue in school or go to work is a momentous decision.

2. Before making a decision, the graduate must consider many things.

3. First of all, finances can be a problem.

4. In making the decision, the availability of jobs becomes a factor.

5. If one decides to go on to college, the selection of a career is important.

6. Next, one should consider academic preparation and the time it may take to complete his education.

7. After that, one must decide which college or university to attend.

8. If necessary, passports and visas must be obtained.

9. For all male students, military service might be a consideration in making a decision.

10. Everything considered, the decision to continue in school or not is a difficult one.

Assignment 3:B

Make yes/no questions from the following sentences. Be sure to move the shifters from the front to the end of each sentence before moving the aux-words.

SPECTATOR SPORTS

1. For many Americans, sports are a reason for living.

2. Every weekend, they sit glued to their chairs watching television.

3. In the spring, the baseball season starts.

4. In the fall, it ends with the world series.

5. By then the football season is well under way.

6. On Saturdays and Sundays, college and pro games often overlap.

7. All day long one can follow the plays and root for favorite teams.

8. On television sports, the best plays can be seen two and three times.

9. After the strenuous games are over, spectators have only to switch off the television and walk a short distance to find food and rest.

10. For anyone who doesn't need exercise, watching sports on television is a great activity.

Assignment 3:C
Make yes/no questions from the following sentences. Be sure to move the shifters from the front to the end of each sentence before moving the aux-words.

WRITING ENGLISH

1. For many students, writing English is their hardest task.

2. Although they like to talk, they dislike writing.

3. If they would learn the basic skills of writing, it wouldn't be so hard.

108 SENTENCE CONSTRUCTION

4. First of all the student must recognize that speaking and writing are different arts.

5. As a starter, a student should learn the verb forms and their particular uses.

6. Along with this, a student needs to learn to substitute correct pronouns.

7. After that he should develop the ability to write simple sentences correctly.

8. If he can do this, it shouldn't be any trouble to learn how to combine sentences.

9. After all the mechanics have been mastered, individual style can be developed.

10. In the end, good sentences make good paragraphs and well written paragraphs become good essays.

4. BASIC SENTENCE PATTERNS

There are four basic sentence patterns in English. All consist of a subject and a predicate. If a **timeless** verb form is used in any pattern it **must** be preceded by an aux-word.

Sentence Pattern Number One

Subject	+	(Aux-word)	+	$Verb_t$	+	Object
My father				loves		my mother.
John		is		watching		television.

Sentence Pattern Number Two

Subject	+	(Aux-word)	+	$Verb_i$
Georgia				giggles.
Mr. Harris		can		come.

Sentence Pattern Number Three

Subject	+	(Aux-word)	+	$Verb_L$	+	Complement
Marianne				seems		tired.
He		might		appear		intelligent.

The Sentence 109

Sentence Pattern Number Four

Subject	+	(Aux-word)	+	be	+	Complement
My rich uncle				is		an old man. (noun)
He		has		been		very sick. (adjective)
His money				is		in stocks and bonds. (prepositional phrase)

Each of these patterns is discussed in more detail later in this chapter.

Assignment 4:A

Write the number of the sentence pattern used (1, 2, 3, or 4) in each sentence below.

TESTS I

_____ 1. I like tests.

_____ 2. They are a lot of fun.

_____ 3. I feel happy when I am taking a test.

_____ 4. This seems strange to most people.

_____ 5. They think that I am crazy.

_____ 6. Tests are challenging.

_____ 7. I study hard before taking a test.

_____ 8. Sometimes I make mistakes.

_____ 9. I learn from my mistakes.

_____ 10. Teachers give tests for many reasons.

_____ 11. Some like to punish students.

_____ 12. Others want to measure their students' knowledge.

_____ 13. My teachers don't know that I like tests.

_____ 14. I don't tell them my secret.

_____ 15. They might not give any more tests to me.

Assignment 4:B

Write the number of the sentence pattern used (1, 2, 3, or 4) in each sentence below.

TESTS II

_____ 1. I hate tests.　　　　　　　　　　_____ 4. I feel sick.

_____ 2. Teachers give tests all the time.　_____ 5. My head spins.

_____ 3. Tests bother me.　　　　　　　　_____ 6. I want to run away.

SENTENCE CONSTRUCTION

_____ 7. I still try hard.

_____ 8. I can't think while taking a test.

_____ 9. Teachers don't understand.

_____ 10. They seem indifferent to my feelings.

_____ 11. They say I must take tests.

_____ 12. I feel worse.

_____ 13. I suffer in silence.

_____ 14. I try everything.

_____ 15. I still fail.

_____ 16. I leave the classroom quietly.

_____ 17. I feel like an idiot.

_____ 18. No one understands me.

_____ 19. Someday they will learn that I am really smart.

_____ 20. I am not as stupid as they think.

Assignment 4:C

Write the number of the sentence pattern used (1, 2, 3, or 4) in each sentence below.

THE WORLD FOOD PROBLEM

_____ 1. Everyone must eat.

_____ 2. Some areas have plenty of food.

_____ 3. In other places food is very scarce.

_____ 4. They don't have enough food to go around.

_____ 5. Food costs vary from place to place.

_____ 6. In some countries a person must spend almost all his wages for food for himself and his family.

_____ 7. And then sometimes they must go without enough to eat.

_____ 8. In other places people spend less than ten percent of their income for food.

_____ 9. Some places grow abundant crops.

_____ 10. Many people appear overfed.

_____ 11. They are overweight.

_____ 12. Some places do not have very much food.

_____ 13. Sometimes people cannot pay for the available food.

_____ 14. People frequently die from starvation.

_____ 15. Many people in the world are concerned about this.

_____ 16. Perhaps something can be done about the world food problem.

5. SENTENCE PATTERN NUMBER ONE

The most commonly used sentence pattern in English is sentence pattern number one.

Subject	+	(Aux-word)	+	Verb$_t$	+	Object
We				admired (time included)		him.
The president		has (time included)		made (timeless)		a promise.
Our team		will (time included)		win (timeless)		the game.

Verbs in pattern number one *must* be followed by an object. They are called *transitive* verbs. In most dictionaries the abbreviation *vt* means the verb is transitive (requires an object).

The following are some common transitive verbs (they usually take objects):

throw	do
set	make
lay	elect
raise	demand
remember	like
have	want
see	bring
thank	try
love	threaten

Assignment 5:A

Write ten simple, related sentences on the topic of **games** *or* **dating**. *Follow basic sentence pattern number one for all of your sentences. Use time-included forms or aux-words and timeless verb forms. Make sure that each sentence is error-free! Put the headings below at the top of your paper.*

Subject	(Aux-word)	Verb (transitive)	Object

Assignment 5:B

Write ten simple, related sentences on the topic of **careers** *or* **politics.** *Follow basic sentence pattern number one for all of your sentences. Use time-included forms or aux-words and timeless verb forms. Make sure that each sentence is error-free! Put the headings below at the top of your paper.*

<u>Subject</u>   <u>(Aux-word)</u>   <u>Verb (transitive)</u>   <u>Object</u>

Assignment 5:C

Write ten simple, related sentences on the topic of **cultures** *or* **marriage.** *Follow basic sentence pattern number one for all of your sentences. Use time-included forms or aux-words and timeless verb forms. Make sure that each sentence is error-free! Put the headings below at the top of your paper.*

<u>Subject</u>   <u>(Aux-word)</u>   <u>Verb (transitive)</u>   <u>Object</u>

6. SENTENCE PATTERN NUMBER TWO

Subject	+	(Aux-word)	+	Verb$_i$
Alexander				travels.
				(time-included)
Profits		should		increase.
		(time-included)		(timeless)

Verbs in this pattern do *not* take objects. They are called *intransitive* verbs. In most dictionaries the abbreviation *vi* means the verb is intransitive.

The following are some common intransitive verbs (they do not usually take objects):

go	sit
lie	rise
come	travel
happen	sleep
live	exist

Note: In this book, transitive and intransitive verbs are defined in terms of **function,** not **meaning.**

Example:

He *throws* the ball. (Sentence pattern number one)
    vt

He *throws* well. (Sentence pattern number two)
    vi

Assignment 6:A

Write ten simple, related sentences on the topic of **exercise** *or* **work**. *Follow basic sentence pattern number two for all of your sentences. Use* time-included *verb forms or* aux-words *and* timeless *verb forms. Make sure that each sentence is error-free! Put the headings below at the top of your paper.*

Subject   (Aux-word)   Verb (intransitive)

Assignment 6:B

Write ten simple, related sentences on the topic of **travel** *or* **death**. *Follow basic sentence pattern number two for all of your sentences. Use* time-included *verb forms or* aux-words *and* timeless *verb forms. Make sure that each sentence is error-free! Put the headings below at the top of your paper.*

Subject   (Aux-word)   Verb (intransitive)

Assignment 6:C

Write ten simple, related sentences on the topic of **time** *or* **study**. *Follow basic sentence pattern number two for all of your sentences. Use* time-included *verb forms or* aux-words *and* timeless *verb forms. Make sure that each sentence is error-free! Put the headings below at the top of your paper.*

Subject   (Aux-word)   Verb (intransitive)

7. TRANSITIVE/INTRANSITIVE VERBS

Some verbs are **transitive and intransitive.**

In other words, they may or may not take objects. They may be used in either sentence pattern number one or pattern number two.

Adverbs* and/or prepositional phrases of place, time, and manner (usually in that order) may be added to any basic sentence (many of these adverbs and phrases function as shifters). Any nouns in these phrases are objects of the preposition and **not** objects of the verb.

Examples:

    vt   He   walked   the dog   yesterday.
                        (vt)   (object)   (adverb)

    vi   He   walked   a mile   yesterday.
                        (vi)   (adverb) (adverb)

    vt   The   policeman   has   stopped   the car.
                                    (aux)   (vt)   (object)

*Adverbs usually answer the questions *when?*, *how?*, and *where?*

SENTENCE CONSTRUCTION

vi   The car stopped.
                               (vi)

vt   I run the movie projector at school every day.
              (vt)   (object)   (adverb)   (adverb)

vi   I run five miles every day.
              (vi)   (adverb)   (adverb)

Assignment 7:A

Copy the passage below. Underline each transitive verb *(or transitive verb group) and write* vt *above it. Circle the complete object of each transitive verb. Underline each* intransitive verb *(or intransitive verb group) and write* vi *above it. The first one has already been done for you.*

A BASEBALL GAME

¹John always enjoys (a good baseball game). ²He attends whenever he has a chance. ³Last night's game thrilled him. ⁴The home team was playing against their biggest rival. ⁵The fans filled the stands. ⁶The home team had been winning. ⁷Then a batter hit a line drive. ⁸The ball hit the pitcher. ⁹It injured his arm. ¹⁰The new pitcher did not have sufficient time to warm up. ¹¹A home run put the other team in the lead. ¹²In the next innning, the pitcher warmed up. ¹³He fanned three batters in a row. ¹⁴In the last inning, the home team rallied. ¹⁵A home run with the bases loaded tipped the score in favor of the home team. ¹⁶John went home happy.

Assignment 7:B

Copy the passage below. Underline each transitive verb *(or transitive verb group) and write* vt *above it. Circle the complete object of each transitive verb. Underline each* intransitive verb *(or intransitive verb group) and write* vi *above it. The first one has already been done for you.*

ORIGAMI

¹Have you ever made (a paper crane?) ²If so, you have encountered the art of origami (Japanese paper folding). ³One must have lots of patience to master this art. ⁴Origami experts must practice for years. ⁵They can easily forget the art.

⁶You may use any kind of paper. ⁷The stiff shiny colored squares make the prettiest folded objects. ⁸However, the real beauty of the object depends on the skill of the folder.

⁹Origami relaxes many people. ¹⁰It comes naturally to them. ¹¹It can drive others crazy! ¹²They can't succeed no matter how hard they try.

Assignment 7:C

Copy the passage below. Underline each transitive verb *(or transitive verb group) and write* vt *above it. Circle the complete object of each transitive verb. Underline each* intransitive verb *(or intransitive verb group) and write* vi *above it. The first one has already been done for you.*

THE GREAT BLIZZARD

¹On the morning of Sunday, March 11, 1888, people in New York City were rushing home from church meetings. ²A cold rain was falling on the city. ³No one expected a great blizzard. ⁴The newspaper had predicted clear weather. ⁵Strange things were happening in the atmosphere. ⁶A body of icy cold air more than 1,000 miles

long was sweeping down from Canada. ⁷It brought freezing temperatures to the entire eastern third of the United States. ⁸The cold front stretched from New England to Florida. ⁹It met a front of warm, wet air from the south. ¹⁰The heavy rain changed to blinding snow. ¹¹Soon hurricane winds were ripping the Eastern seaboard. ¹²The storm struck Washington, D.C. ¹³It buried the capital with snow. ¹⁴The violent winds smashed ships near the shore onto the rocky coast.

¹⁵On Monday morning, thousands of New York workers left their homes. ¹⁶They were going to work. ¹⁷Most of them did not make it. ¹⁸Some could not even open their front doors. ¹⁹Snow drifts thirty to forty feet high paralyzed the city. ²⁰They even stopped the trains. ²¹Many people acted like heroes that day. ²²They rescued others from the snow and cold.

²³By Wednesday the storm had ended. ²⁴By the next Sunday most of the snow had melted. ²⁵Life was returning to normal. ²⁶The eastern United States had weathered the greatest blizzard in American history.

Assignment 7.1:A

Write ten simple, related sentences on the topic of **sports.** *Follow either basic sentence pattern number one or basic sentence pattern number two for each of your sentences. Use time-included verb forms or aux-words and timeless verb forms. Make sure that each sentence is error-free! Write* vt *above each transitive verb and* circle *its object. Write* vi *above each intransitive verb.*

Assignment 7.1:B

Write ten simple, related sentences on the topic of **humor.** *Follow either basic sentence pattern number one or basic sentence pattern number two for each of your sentences. Use time-included verb forms or aux-words and timeless verb forms. Make sure that each sentence is error-free! Write* vt *above each transitive verb and* circle *its object. Write* vi *above each intransitive verb.*

Assignment 7.1:C

Write ten, simple related sentences on the topic of **geography.** *Follow either basic sentence pattern number one or basic sentence pattern number two for each of your sentences. Use time-included verb forms or aux-words and timeless verb forms. Make sure that each sentence is error-free! Write* vt *above each transitive verb and* circle *its object. Write* vi *above each intransitive verb.*

8. SENTENCE PATTERN NUMBER THREE

Subject	+	(Aux-word)	+	Verb$_L$	+	Complement
Those men				look (time included)		happy. (adjective)
The food		should (time-included)		taste (timeless)		delicious. (adjective)
The steak				tastes (time-included)		like cardboard (*like* + noun)
It				appears (time-included)		to be tender (*to* + verb)

8.1 Verbs used in this pattern are called **linking verbs** because they connect the subject and the complement.

The following are some common linking verbs (they take adjective complements).

    seem   appear
    smell   look
    feel   sound
    taste   become (may also take a noun complement)
             get

116 SENTENCE CONSTRUCTION

8.2 Linking verbs are intransitive. When these verbs are used with an object their meaning changes. (They are then used in pattern number one.)

Examples:

    vt   I smell the food. (pattern number one)
            (vt)   (object)

    vL   The food smells good. (pattern number three)
                 (vL) (adj) (The food is not doing the smelling.)

    vt   I feel the sandpaper. (pattern number one)
            (vt)   (object)

    vL   The sandpaper feels rough. (pattern number three)
                      (vL) (adj) (The sandpaper is not doing the feeling.)

8.3 When *like* follows the linking verb, noun complements may also be used.

Example:

    This steak tastes like cardboard.

8.4 *to* + verb phrases (explained in Chapter 13) may also follow some linking verbs (such as, *seem* and *appear*).

Example:

    He seems to be tired.

Assignment 8:A

Write ten simple, related sentences about **a place where people eat.** *Follow basic sentence pattern number three for all of your sentences. Use time-included verb forms or aux-words with timeless verb forms. Make sure that each sentence is error-free!* Put the headings below at the top of your paper.

Subject	(Aux-word)	Verb (linking)	Adjective

Assignment 8:B

Write ten simple, related sentences about **a place where people dance.** *Follow basic sentence pattern number three for all of your sentences. Use time-included verb forms or aux-words with timeless verb forms. Make sure that each sentence is error-free!* Put the headings below at the top of your paper.

Subject	(Aux-word)	Verb (linking)	Adjective

Assignment 8:C

Write ten simple, related sentences about **a person you know well.** *Follow basic sentence pattern number three for all of your sentences. Use time-included verb forms or aux-words with timeless verb forms. Make sure that each sentence is error-free!* Put the headings below at the top of your paper.

Subject	(Aux-word)	Verb (linking)	Adjective

9. SENTENCE PATTERN NUMBER FOUR

Subject	+	Aux-word *be*	+	Complement
Dr. Rogers		is		a surgeon. (noun)
The elephants		are		enormous. (adjective)
The students		are		in the library. (prepositional phrase)*

Note that there are three possible kinds of complements—*nouns, adjectives,* or *prepositional phrases.*

Additional aux-words may also be used. In these cases the form of *be* is determined by the preceding aux-word.

Subject	+	Aux-word	+	be	+	Complement
That man		may (time-included)		be (timeless)		the thief. (noun)
That dog		might (time-included)		be (timeless)		sick. (adj)
Jack		could (time-included)		be (timeless)		in the bookstore. (prep. phrase)
My grandfather		has (time-included)		been (timeless)		a doctor for many years. (noun + adverb)
George		has (time-included)		been (timeless)		sick. (adj)
They		have (time-included)		been (timeless)		at home. (prep. phrase)
Jeannette		is** (time-included)		being** (timeless)		funny. (adj)

Note: A noun complement is **not** the same as an object. In fact, it is essentially the same thing as the subject. (Subject pronouns are used in complement position.)

Objects and subjects are **not** related except by the action of the verb.

*the locatives *here, there, home, anywhere,* and *everywhere* may be substituted for the prepositional phrase complement.

**rarely used

Assignment 9:A

Write twelve simple, related sentences about **a famous person.** *Follow* **basic** *sentence pattern number four for all of your sentences. Use* **noun** *complements in four sentences,* **adjective** *complements in four sentences, and* **prepositional phrase** *complements in four sentences. Label each sentence* N, A, *or* P *depending on the kind of complement you use. Make sure that each sentence is error-free.*

Assignment 9:B

Write twelve simple, related sentences about **a famous place.** *Follow* **basic** *sentence pattern number four for all of your sentences. Use* **noun** *complements in four sentences,* **adjective** *complements in four sentences, and* **prepositional phrase** *complements in four sentences. Label each sentence* N, A, *or* P *depending on the kind of complement you use. Make sure that each sentence is error-free.*

Assignment 9:C

Write twelve simple, related sentences about **a famous thing.** *Follow* **basic** *sentence pattern number four for all of your sentences. Use* **noun** *complements in four sentences,* **adjective** *complements in four sentences, and* **prepositional phrase** *complements in four sentences. Label each sentence* N, A, *or* P *depending on the kind of complement you use. Make sure that each sentence is error-free.*

10. SUMMARY OF SENTENCE PATTERNS

10.1 The four sentence patterns presented in this chapter are the basic sentence patterns in English.

Pattern 1.	Subject	(Aux-word)	Transitive Verb	Object
	John		drinks	milk.
	John	will	drink	milk.

Pattern 2.	Subject	(Aux-word)	Intransitive Verb	
	John		works.	
	John	can	work.	

Pattern 3.	Subject	(Aux-word)	Linking Verb	Complement
	John		seems	content.
	John	has	seemed	content.

Pattern 4.	Subject	(Aux-word)	be	Complement
	John		is	a doctor.
	John	could	be	a doctor.

All other sentences are *variations, transformations,* or *combinations* of these basic patterns.

10.2 One common variation is the addition of a noun, adjective, or verb complement to an object (sentence pattern number one). This complement describes or shows the action of the **object,** not the subject, of the sentence.

Examples:

Subject	+	Vt	+	Object	+	Complement
Barbara		called		Stephen		a coward. (noun complement)
The PTA		appointed		John		chairman. (noun complement)
The students		made		Sally		embarrassed. (adjective complement)
They		painted		their house		yellow. (adjective complement)
That movie		made		me		cry. (verb complement)
We		heard		the dogs		bark(ing). (verb complement)

Note that **only timeless base and -*ing* verb forms are used as verb complements** (*d-t-n* verb forms may be used as adjectives). Time-included verb forms are never used as complements to objects.

10.3 The passive and indirect object **transformations** are discussed in Chapter 10. However, here are a couple of examples:

   John was hit by a car. (Passive formed from pattern no. 1: A car hit John.)
   John gave Mary a present. (Indirect object transformation from pattern no. 1: John gave a present to Mary.)

10.4 Combinations are discussed in Book II.
However, here are examples of three common sentence combinations.

1. Snow White married Prince Charming and they lived happily ever after. (From sentence pattern no. 1, "Snow White married Prince Charming," and sentence pattern no. 2, "They lived happily ever after.")
2. Although the weather was fine, they stayed home. (From sentence pattern no. 4, "The weather was fine," and sentence pattern no. 2, "They stayed home.")
3. Jumping up from his seat, George shook his fist at the man. (From sentence pattern no. 2, "George jumped up," and sentence pattern no. 1, "George shook his fist at the man.")

10.5 *Inversions* are rarely used in speech, but are often found in formal writing.

When inversions are used, sentence units do not follow their normal order.

Examples:
>Never realized was Dorothy's ambition to become a movie star.
>Dorothy's ambition to become a movie star was never realized. (normal)
>
>Strange though my story may seem, it is true.
>Though my story may seem strange, it is true. (normal)
>
>Eligible to apply for the awards are graduating high school seniors.
>Graduating high school seniors are eligible to apply for the awards. (normal)

The rules for these inversions are very complex and depend on a number of factors such as vocabulary, emphasis, original sentence construction, register, and style. It is not recommended that you use them in your writing at this stage, and they will not be explained in this book. However, you should be able to recognize inversions when you see them in writing.

Assignment 10:A

Using only *the four basic sentence patterns (and the complement variation if you wish), but* no *transformations or combinations, write fifteen error-free, related sentences about* **your home or room.** *Use each of the four basic sentence patterns at least once. Label your sentences (1), (2), (3), or (4) according to the basic sentence pattern you choose to use.*

Assignment 10:B

Using only *the four basic sentence patterns (and the complement variation if you wish), but* no *transformations or combinations, write fifteen error-free, related sentences about* **a town or city.** *Use each of the four basic sentence patterns at least once. Label your sentences (1), (2), (3), or (4) according to the basic sentence pattern you choose to use.*

Assignment 10:C

Using only *the four basic sentence patterns (and the complement variation if you wish), but* no *transformations or combinations, write fifteen error-free, related sentences about* **your best friend or worst enemy.** *Use each of the four basic sentence patterns at least once. Label your sentences (1), (2), (3), or (4) according to the basic sentence pattern you choose to use.*

11. *WH-* QUESTIONS

11.1 *Wh-* questions are sometimes called **information** questions because they require more than a simple *yes* or *no* answer. They are called *wh-* questions because they begin with the question words *who, whom, what, which, where, when, why, whose,* or *how*. Only one of these *wh-* words can be used at a time when forming a question from a basic sentence (which contains the answer to the question).

There are two main *wh-* question patterns:

1. Questions about the **subject** of the sentence, and
2. Questions about **objects or other parts of the predicate** of the sentence.

11.2 Subject Question Pattern

If the subject of the basic sentence is **human,** simply substitute *who* for the complete subject whether it is singular or plural. When a **plural** subject is replaced by *who* or *what,* it is common to change the aux-word or verb to its singular form (*-s* form) unless the rest of the sentence indicates that the replaced subject is plural.

120   SENTENCE CONSTRUCTION

Examples:

John gave my books to Mary. (basic sentence)
Who gave my books to Mary? (*wh-* question) (answer = John)

The boys at the bus stop were waiting impatiently. (basic sentence)
Who was waiting impatiently? (*wh-* question) (answer = The boys at the bus stop)

If the subject is **non-human,** simply substitute *what* for the complete subject whether it is singular or plural (and, if the replaced subject is plural, change the aux-word or verb to its singular form).

Examples:

The morning newspaper carried *a notice of the meeting* on the last page.
What carried a notice of the meeting on the last page?

The trees in the park shaded the picnic area.
What shaded the picnic area?

11.3   Predicate Question Pattern

In this pattern the **aux-word** must be moved in front of the subject as it is for yes/no questions. (This is explained in Chapter 4.) The *wh-* word replaces the complete object or other part of the predicate, but it is placed before the aux-word.

If the object is **human,** the *wh-* word is *whom.* (*Whom* is rarely used in speech, but it is common in formal writing.)

If the object is **non-human,** the *wh-* word is *what.*

Examples:

Dr. Anderson addressed *the students* in the assembly.
Whom did Dr. Anderson *address* in the assembly?
(*wh-*) (hidden aux-word) (base form)

The morning newspaper carried *a notice of the meeting on the last page.*
What did the morning newspaper *carry* on the last page?
(*wh-*) (hidden aux-word)   (base form)

Other *wh-* question words used as substitutes for other parts of the predicate are:
   where for place
   when for time
   why for purpose or reason
   how for manner (also *how much* and *how many* for quantity)
   whose for possessives (the accompanying noun is also moved to the front of the sentence)

As with the *whom* or *what* replacement, these *wh-* words are placed at the beginning of the sentence followed by the aux-word.

Examples:

John gave my books to Mary *in front of the library.* (place)
Where did John give my books to Mary?

John gave my books to Mary *after school.* (time)
When did John give my books to Mary?

John *quickly* gave my books to Mary. (manner)
How did John give my books to Mary?

John gave my books to Mary *because he had to catch the bus.* (reason)
Why did John give my books to Mary?

John gave *my* books to Mary. (possessive)
Whose books did John give to Mary?

When the word being replaced by the *wh-* word is the **object of a preposition**, *whom* (for humans) or *what* (for non-humans) is used. In formal usage, the preposition is also moved to the front and precedes the *wh-* word.

Example:

    John gave my books *to Mary*. (preposition and object of preposition)
    To whom did John give my books?

The word *which* is used when **choosing from a group** of people or things. It is often followed by the word *of* and a plural noun. (Although the noun is plural, the aux-word or verb agrees with the singular *which*.)

Examples:

    Here are some new styles. *Which* do you prefer?

    Which of these books is yours?

How is often followed by other adjectives to ask special information questions (e.g., *how far* for distance, *how hot* for temperature, *how old* for age, etc.).

What occasionally replaces adjectives in forming questions (e.g., *what color, what building*).

Assignment 11:A

Make up an exam about the following passage by substituting wh- *words for the underlined parts of each sentence. You may use pronouns in your questions. Write your seventeen questions on a separate sheet of paper.*

A RADIO DRAMA

<u>Many people</u> were listening to a <u>radio program</u> <u>one evening in 1938</u>. <u>This program</u> was broadcast <u>before
     1   2   3   4
television sets were common household furniture.</u> <u>People</u> heard <u>reports</u> <u>that men from outer space had landed
                    5   6   7
in the state of New Jersey.</u> <u>The program</u> announced <u>when it started, and again when it ended,</u> <u>that the
                                   8   9
men-from-space landing was completely fictitious.</u> <u>Panic-stricken people</u> crowded narrow highways and
                      10   11
tunnels <u>in New Jersey</u> <u>that evening</u>. They were trying to escape <u>the fictional invasion</u>. <u>Orson Welles</u> was <u>the
        12   13   14   15
producer of this extraordinary program.</u> Even today, he is remembered for <u>this action-packed radio drama</u>.
             16   17

Assignment 11:B

Make up an exam about the following passage by substituting wh- *words for the underlined parts of each sentence. You may use pronouns in your questions. Write your seventeen questions on a separate sheet of paper.*

FLEET FEET

<u>Many</u> fast <u>running</u> animals live <u>in the wilderness areas of the world</u>. <u>Gazelles, cheetahs, and antelope</u> all
    1   2   3
attain <u>high speeds</u> <u>while running</u>. <u>The fastest running animal of them all</u> is <u>the fleet-footed cheetah</u>. A <u>cheetah</u>
         4   5   6   7   8
can run <u>seventy-one miles per hour</u> <u>as it flees from an enemy</u>. <u>The fast running cheetah</u> can attain a forty-five
         9   10   11
mile-an-hour speed within <u>two</u> seconds from a standing start <u>on the plains</u>. <u>The best cars</u> cannot match <u>that fast
                                 12   13   14   15
start</u> <u>on racing days</u> at the racetrack.
    16   17

SENTENCE CONSTRUCTION

Assignment 11:C

Make up an exam about the following passage by substituting wh- words for the underlined parts of each sentence. You may use pronouns in your questions. Write your sixteen questions on a separate sheet of paper.

KING TUT'S TOMB

In 1922, an English archaeologist named Howard Carter was working near Cairo, Egypt. He looked through a small hole that he had drilled in the wall of a tomb. At first, he saw nothing. Then, as his eyes grew accustomed to the light, he began to distinguish the details of the room. He saw strange animals, statues, and gold—everywhere the glint of gold! He had discovered the tomb of Tutankhamen, one of the great Pharaohs of ancient Egypt. A clay tablet in the tomb carried the inscription "Death will slay with his wings whoever disturbs the peace of the Pharaoh."

Since 1922, many scientists, archaeologists, and scholars who have worked with King Tut's relics have suffered misfortunes. Over thirty of these people have died. Many people claim that "King Tut's curse" is responsible for every one of these misfortunes. Others do not take the "curse" quite so seriously.

8
MODIFIERS

1. THE NUCLEUS OF THE NOUN PHRASE

Every subject or object noun phrase has one main noun. In this book it is called the *nucleus*.

Verbs, aux-words, and pronouns agree with this nucleus (or main noun).

Other words may be used to modify the nucleus. The resulting group of words is not a sentence, but a noun phrase. Words used to modify nouns are usually called adjectives. Words used to modify verbs and other modifiers are usually called adverbs. The forms of adjectives and adverbs are explained in Chapter 1.

2. ORDER OF NOUN MODIFIERS

2.1   Single-word modifiers precede the nucleus.

Examples:

>   The globe.
>   The world globe.
>   The large world globe.
> The large multi-colored world globe.

2.2   When more than one single-word modifier is used, they follow a set order. See the chart on page 125 for this order. This order is changed only when special emphasis is given to one modifier. In writing, an emphasized out-of-place modifier should be underlined (italicized).

2.3   When the nucleus is a **singular count noun** or **group noun,** one (and only one) of the following modifiers must be used: an article (explained in Chapter 2), a demonstrative, a possessive, or the word *one*.

With **noncount** or **plural count nouns** articles, demonstratives, or possessives may or may not be used. (The demonstratives *this* and *that* and the articles *a/an, each,* and *every* are used only to modify singular nouns.

2.4   All single word modifiers do **not** always modify the nucleus. They may modify other modifiers.
      The South American businessman

In this noun phrase, *South* modifes *American,* while the combination *South American* modifies the nucleus *businessman.*

2.5 When two or more single-word, nucleus modifiers (in columns III to VII on the chart) occur together, they are usually separated by commas.

A simple test to determine if a comma is needed is to place the word *and* between the two adjectives. If *and* can be used, then the comma is correct.

Examples:
   The four little (and) brown rocks
   The four little, brown rocks

   The least difficult algebra problem
   (because *least* modifies *difficult,* no comma is used)

Assignment 1:A

Rewrite the following passage on a separate sheet of paper. Copy the sentences as they are, but rearrange the modifiers (in parentheses) into their proper order.

A DANGEROUS VOYAGE

[1] Last year, (cold, water-soaked, five, tired) men battled (storm-tossed, Atlantic, the, dangerous) ocean in (leather, a, fragile, small) vessel to prove that (Atlantic, northern, ancient, an) voyage could have been made. [2] (adventurous, brave, the) crew of (leather, small, the) craft successfully sailed across (perilous, the, icy, northern, Atlantic) ocean despite (the, ice, large) floes and (rocky, hazardous, the) shorelines. [3] (heroic, this, superhuman) feat once again shows us that man can battle (hostile, unknown, an) environment and win.

Assignment 1:B

Rewrite the following passage. Copy the sentences as they are, but rearrange the modifiers (in parentheses) into their proper order.

THE WORLD SERIES

[1] I saw (series, first, baseball, my, world) game (Tuesday, last) night. [2] (two-acre, modern, the, ball) park provided the fans with (folding, many, comfortable) seats, but (thrilling, the, most) thing was (action-packed, fast-moving, the) game itself. [3] (first, talented, the) baseman played (outstanding, very, a, ball) game. [4] (Yankee, hard-hitting, the, baseball) players played (errorless, exciting, an, three-hour) game. [5] (single, the, outstanding) play of (world, that, sports) event was (single-handed, unbelievable, an) catch by (third, the, dependable) baseman. [6] This prevented (game-winning, certain, a) home run by (losing, home, the) team, as (exuberant, Yankee, the, winning, team) members were cheered by (excited, cheering, the, Yankee, out-of-state) fans. [7] (baseball, one, this, series, thrilling, world) game has made me (lifetime, a, baseball) fan.

Assignment 1:C

Rewrite the following passage. Copy the sentences as they are, but rearrange the modifiers (in parentheses) into their proper order.

RECORDS

[1] For (strange, any, fantastic) facts about records, consult (gigantic, amazing, new, the) edition of the *Guinness Book of Records*. [2] It is (reliable, best-known, the, international, reference) book available for (authentic, the, record-breaking) achievements of men and women. [3] It lists (natural, fantastic, many) phenomena, such as (known, the, greatest, volcanic) explosion, (most, known, active, southerly, the) volcano, (lava, longest, the) flow, and (prehistoric, the, known, lava, largest) flow. [4] In addition, (racing, fastest, world's, the) car, (production, fastest, the) cars, and (powerful, most, piston-engined, world's, the) car are also named.

Modifiers

ORDER OF NOUN MODIFIERS

	SINGLE WORD MODIFIERS							NOUN	PHRASES AND CLAUSES	
I	II	III	IV	V	VI	VII	VIII	NUCLEUS	IX	X
Pre-article	1. Articles and Indefinite adjectives 2. Demonstratives 3. Possessives	Numerals 1. Ordinal 2. Cardinal	Superlative and Comparative Markers	1. General Size 2. Quality or Characteristic 3. General Weight	1. Specific Size 2. Shape 3. Age 4. Temperature 5. Specific Weight	1. Time 2. Color 3. Location 4. Origin or Nationality	Nouns used as Adjectives		Modifying Phrases	Modifying Clauses
both	the			tired	old	Indian	algebra	men	sitting there	
Only	the		least	difficult				problem		that we did
	The	first two						chapters	in the book	
	These	four		little		brown		rocks		
	Her	first			new			job		
	John's		less	surprising			application	attitude		
	The man's			impressive	six-foot	blue	plastic	form		
	My brother's		more	big	rectangular	black	picture	chair	from New York	that you saw
	Many			expensive	cold	Alaskan	winter	frames		
	A	Six				American		day		
				rich			news	tourists	carrying cameras	who talk loudly
	Those					weekly		magazines		which came today
All	the	twenty	most	beautiful	new	red	water	beds	with leaks	that I fixed

Note: Only one modifier from column II can be used at a time.
If the nucleus is singular, then a modifier from column II must be used.
If the nucleus is plural, then a modifier from column II may or may not be used.

3. SINGULAR AND PLURAL FORMS OF MODIFIERS

Only the demonstratives have singular and plural forms. All other modifiers have only one form—*singular*—although they may be used with singular or plural nouns.

Examples:

This ruler is two *feet* long.	It is a two-*foot* ruler.
The boy is three *years* old.	He is a three-*year*-old boy.
The building is forty *stories* high.	It is a forty-*story* building.

Note: A hyphen is normally used between each of the words in a group of words which acts as a single modifier.

4. THE MODIFIER *VERY*

Very is an intensifying adverb. It is used to modify adjectives and other adverbs. *Very* cannot be used to modify *nouns*.

Examples:

She is tall.	She is very tall.
The large man is my uncle.	The very large man is my uncle.

5. ADJECTIVE COMPLEMENT MODIFIERS

When an adjective complement (sentence pattern number four) forms part of one or more related sentences with a nucleus noun in common, the sentences may be *combined* by using the adjective complements as single-word modifiers.

Examples:

The room was dark. The room scared Sheila.	The dark room scared Sheila.
The trees were green. The trees were beautiful. They cut down the trees.	They cut down the beautiful green trees.

Assignment 5:A

Change the sentences under each main sentence into single-word adjectives. Place these adjectives in the main sentence before the nouns they modify. Then write the modified sentences in paragraph form.

ATHLETICS

1. Fans admire an athlete.
   The fans are sports-minded.
   The athlete is successful.
2. However, people realize the effort required to succeed in the field of athletics.
   The people are few.
   The effort is tremendous.
   The field is competitive.
3. Athletes must forgo pleasures.
   The athletes are great.
   The pleasures are many.
4. They must develop self-discipline.
   The self-discipline is great.

5. A training period is not unusual.
   The training period is intensive.
   The training period is six months.
6. They spend hours in exercise.
   The hours are countless.
   The exercise is grueling.
7. They must eat food.
   The food is nutritious.
8. Cooperation with coaches is vital for success.
   The cooperation is constant.
   The coaches are different.
   The success is athletic.
9. An athlete must develop a spirit.
   The athlete is dedicated.
   The spirit is competitive.
10. Success in sports is achieved only through effort.
    The sports are competitive.
    The effort is constant.
    The effort is consistent.

Assignment 5:B

Change the sentences under each main sentence into single-word adjectives. Place these adjectives in the main sentence before the nouns they modify. Then write the modified sentences in paragraph form.

AN ESSAY

1. To write an essay, one must begin with sentences.
   The essay is acceptable.
   The essay is two pages.
   The sentences are basic.
2. Sentences require words in syntax.
   The sentences are good.
   The sentences are basic.
   The syntax is correct.
3. Sentences are then combined into paragraphs.
   The sentences are related.
   The paragraphs are topical.
4. Essays depend on sentences.
   The essays are well written.
   The sentences are error-free.
5. Students recognize this.
   The students are good.
6. Students learn to write sentences.
   The students are conscientious.
   The sentences are correct.
   The sentences are grammatical.
7. Then they learn ways to combine their sentences.
   The ways are different.
   The sentences are supporting.

128   SENTENCE CONSTRUCTION

8. They center each paragraph around a sentence.
   The paragraphs are individual.
   The sentences are topic.
9. All material is eliminated.
   The material is extraneous.
10. Paragraphs make essays.
    The paragraphs are informative.
    The essays are interesting.

Assignment 5:C

Change the sentences under each main sentence into single-word adjectives. Place these adjectives in the main sentence before the nouns they modify. Then write the modified sentences in paragraph form.

A GARDEN

1. The gardener receives rewards.
   The gardener is an amateur.
   The rewards are many.
2. A garden makes a yard.
   The garden is lovely.
   The yard is nice-looking.
3. Vegetables for meals are a bonus.
   The vegetables are fresh.
   The meals are healthful.
   The bonus is great.
4. A bouquet of flowers for a house is another bonus.
   The bouquet is lovely.
   The house is well kept.
   The bonus is fine.
5. These benefits do not come without effort.
   The benefits are good.
   The effort is great.
6. The gardener makes sacrifices.
   The gardener is successful.
   The sacrifices are many.
7. Effort is necessary to raise a garden.
   The effort is persistent.
   The garden is good.
8. Watering and weeding are chores.
   The watering and weeding are constant.
   The chores are necessary.
9. There is warfare against bugs.
   The warfare is continual.
   The bugs are plant-destroying.
   The bugs are voracious.
10. The gardener feels that the satisfaction more than compensates for the effort to raise a garden.
    The gardener is successful.
    The satisfaction is personal.
    The garden is successful.
    The effort lasts four months.

6. VERB FORMS USED AS MODIFIERS

6.1 The timeless *d-t-n* and *-ing* forms of many (but not all) verbs are often used as *adjectives*. In these cases they are *not* verbs and are *not* preceded by aux-words.

6.2 The *-ing* form is used as an adjective to describe the *subject* of the basic sentence.

	Basic Sentence	Noun Phrase
Sentence Pattern Number One	*The class* bores the students. (subject)	The boring class
Sentence Pattern Number Two	*The boy* runs. (subject)	The running boy
Sentence Pattern Number One	*The boy* loves the girl. (subject)	The loving boy

6.3 The *d-t-n* form is used as an adjective to describe the *object* of the basic sentence.

	Basic Sentence	Noun Phrase
Sentence Pattern Number One	The class bores the *students*. (object)	The bored students
Sentence Pattern Number One	The boy loves the *girl*. (object)	The loved girl

6.4 Noun phrases containing either *-ing* or *d-t-n* verb form modifiers (formed from basic sentences, as explained in 6.2 and 6.3 above) can be used in any noun position.

Examples:

The boring class had only a few students.
    (subject)

Few students attended *the boring class*.
                    (object)

Dietetics 679 was *a boring class*.
              (complement)

Only a few students made it through *the boring class*.
                              (object of preposition)

The bored students suffered through the class.
    (subject)

The professor ignored *the bored students*.
                       (object)

I was *a bored student*.
       (complement)

Assignment 6:A

Using the methods explained in sections 5 and 6, change the following sentences into noun phrases which contain adjectives. You will not write sentences, so do not use periods.

EMPLOYERS AND EMPLOYEES

1. The work interests the men.

2. The work is hard.

130 SENTENCE CONSTRUCTION

3. The work tires the employees.

4. The employers are helpful.

5. The employees work hard.

6. The employers pay the workers.

7. The workers are busy.

8. The employees deserve praise.

9. The employers praise the employees.

10. The employer-employee team is harmonious.

Assignment 6:B

Using the methods explained in sections 5 and 6, change the following sentences into noun phrases which contain adjectives. You will not write sentences, so do not use periods.

THE THEATRE

1. The performance thrills the audience.

2. The dancers dazzle the viewers.

3. The costumes disgust the critics.

4. The program confuses the readers.

5. The music soothes the listeners.

6. The atmosphere is pleasant.

7. The bright lights illuminate the stage.

8. The actors perform well.

9. The play interests the audience.

10. The show pleases the people.

Assignment 6:C

Using the methods explained in sections 5 and 6, change the following sentences into noun phrases which contain adjectives. You will not write sentences, so do not use periods.

ELECTIONS

1. Elections come in November.

2. The people choose a president.

3. Many candidates vie for office.

4. The candidates harangue the populace.

5. The people suffer the speeches in silence.

6. The voters declare the choice.

7. One candidate wins.

8. Other candidates lose.

9. The voters select another president.

10. Four years later, the procedure is repeated.

7. COMPARATIVE FORMS OF ADJECTIVES

7.1 Adjectives and adverbs are used to describe qualities.

When two things share a common quality, it is possible to compare them.

Comparative forms of adjectives are used to make these comparisons.

Example:

(trees that share a common characteristic: tallness)

This tree is tall.   That tree is taller.

This comparative form is used only to compare *two* things although either one or both of them may be a *group*.

That tree is tall.   Those trees are taller.

7.2 These comparative sentences can be combined into one sentence by using the word *than*. (The predicate in the second sentence is usually deleted. However, the aux-word may be retained.)

Examples:

That tree is taller than this tree (is tall).
He is taller than I am (tall).

Subjective pronouns are used when *subjects* are compared.

Objective pronouns are used when *objects* are compared.

Examples:

John loves Mary.   John loves Mary more than *me*.
John loves me.   (object comparison)

John loves Mary.   John loves Mary more than *I* (do).
I love Mary.   (subject comparison)

7.3   Comparative forms are made by adding the suffix *-er* to one-syllable adjectives.

Examples:

> Last week's test was hard. This week's test was *harder.*
> Bill is fat. John is *fatter.* (notice the double consonant)

The word *more* is placed before adjectives of *three or more* syllables.

Example:

> Last week's test was difficult. This week's test was *more* difficult.

Many (but *not all*) two-syllable adjectives may add *-er* or use the word *more* to make the comparative form.

Example:

> Last week's test was tricky. This week's test was *trickier.* OR
> This week's test was *more tricky.*

Note: Only one of these two methods (*more* or *-er*) may be used at a time.

d-t-n forms and *-ing* forms (discussed in section three of this chapter) used as adjectives always use *more* for comparison.

Examples:

> This class is *more interesting* than that one.
> David is *more bored* than his brother.

There are a few irregular comparative forms of adjectives.

> The comparative form for *good* is *better.*
> The comparative form for *bad* is *worse.*
> The comparative form for *little* is *less.*
> The comparative form for *much* (noncount nouns) is *more.*
> The comparative form for *many* (count nouns) is also *more.*

Assignment 7:A

Answer the following questions with an answer that gives a comparison. Use a different comparison for each question. Be sure that your answer makes sense and that you compare the same sorts of things.

Models:

> Was the lesson long?   It was longer than the last one.
> Was the subject interesting?   It was more interesting than most subjects.

1. Is English difficult?

2. Is writing English easy?

3. Are the grammar rules complex?

4. Is the word order complicated?

5. Are the vocabulary words hard?

6. Is your pronunciation bad?

7. Do you practice often?

8. Is your text good?

9. Is your teacher prepared?

Assignment 7:B

Answer the following questions with an answer that gives a comparison. Use a different comparison for each question. Be sure that your answer makes sense and that you compare the same sorts of things.

Models:

    Was the lesson long?   It was longer than the last one.
    Was the subject interesting?   It was more interesting than most subjects.

1. Was the football game tough?

2. Did the players seem rough?

3. Was the field wet?

4. Did the coach keep calm?

5. Were the winners happy?

6. Were the losers angry?

7. Were the referees fair?

8. Was the stadium full?

Modifiers   135

9. Were the spectators interested?

10. Were the cheerleaders peppy?

Assignment 7:C

Answer the following questions with an answer that gives comparison. Use a different comparison for each question. Be sure that your answer makes sense and that you compare the same sorts of things.

Models:
    Was the lesson long?   It was longer than the last one.
    Was the subject interesting?   It was more interesting than most subjects.

1. Is the country green?

2. Is the country hot?

3. Are the towns small?

4. Are the people happy?

5. Are the roads bad?

6. Is the scenery beautiful?

7. Is the water warm?

8. Are the mountains rugged?

9. Is the harbor deep?

10. Is food plentiful?

8. SUPERLATIVE FORMS OF ADJECTIVES

8.1 Superlative forms of adjectives are used to indicate that one of a group of things exceeds all other things in that group in a specific quality.

The word *the* normally precedes the superlative forms of adjectives.

Examples:

This is the tallest tree in the forest.
Susan is the smartest girl in the class.

8.2 The reference group is not always stated in the sentence, but it must be clear to the reader either from the context or a previous reference.

Examples:

There are many smart girls in our class. Susan is the smartest. (of the class)
This is the hardest test we've had all semester. (of all the tests during the semester)

The superlative forms are made by adding the suffix *-est* to one-syllable adjectives.

8.3 The word *most* is placed before adjectives of three or more syllables.

Many (but *not all*) two-syllable adjectives may add *-est* or use the word *most* to make the superlative form.

Examples:

The tallest inhabited building in the world is the Sears Tower in Chicago.
This is the most interesting book I have ever read.

Assignment 8:A

Study the data below. Then write ten sentences using comparatives and five sentences using superlatives based on the data. (Remember that the *is usually used before the names of bridges. The use of articles with proper nouns is explained in Chapter 2, Section 6 and Chapter 8, Section 2.3).*

THE WORLD'S LONGEST BRIDGE SPANS
A PROGRESSIVE RECORD

Span length in feet	Name	Crosses	Location	Type	Date of Completion
121			Martorell, Spain	Stone Arch	219 B.C.
142	Trajan's Bridge	Nera River	Lucca, Italy	Stone Arch	14 A.D.
170		Danube River		Timber Arch	104
251			Trezzo, Italy	Stone Arch	1377
390			Wettingen, Switzerland	Timber Arch	1758
408	Schuylkill Falls Bridge	Schuylkill River	Philadelphia, Pa., U.S.A.	Suspension	1816
580		Menai Straits	Wales	Chain	1826
1,043	Lewiston Bridge	Niagara River	New York, U.S.A.	Suspension	1851
1,595	Brooklyn Bridge	East River	New York City, U.S.A.	Suspension	1883
1,850	Ambassador Bridge	Detroit River	Detroit, Mich., U.S.A. to Windsor, Canada	Suspension	1929
3,500	George Washington Bridge	Hudson River	New York City, U.S.A.	Suspension	1931
4,200	Golden Gate Bridge	San Francisco Bay	San Francisco, U.S.A.	Suspension	1937
4,260	Verrazano-Narrows Bridge	Entrance to New York Harbor	New York City, U.S.A.	Suspension	1964
4,626	Humber Estuary Bridge	Humber Estuary	England	Suspension	1979

Assignment 8:B

Study the data below. Then write ten sentences using comparatives and five sentences using superlatives based on the data.

INFORMATION ON THE PLANETS

	Mercury	Venus	Earth	Mars	Jupiter	Saturn	Uranus	Neptune	Pluto
Average Distance from the sun (million miles)	36.0	67.2	92.9	141.5	483.4	886.0	1,782	2,792	3,664
Equatorial Diameter (miles)	3,100	7,700	7,927	4,220	88,100	75,100	29,200	27,700	8,700
Mean Orbital Velocity (miles per second)	29.76	21.78	18.52	14.49	8.1	6.0	4.2	3.4	3.0
Mean Surface Gravity	.36	.87	1.00	.38	2.64	1.13	1.07	1.41	——

Assignment 8:C

Study the data below. Then write ten sentences using comparatives and five sentences using superlatives based on the data. (Remember that the *is not usually used before the names of cities and countries.)*

THE WORLD'S LARGEST CITIES

1970			1985 (projected)	
1. New York	16.3	1.	Tokyo	25.2
2. Tokyo	14.9	2.	New York	18.8
3. London	10.5	3.	Mexico City	17.9
4. Shanghai	10.0	4.	Sao Paulo	16.8
5. Mexico City	8.4	5.	Shanghai	14.3
6. Los Angeles	8.4	6.	Los Angeles	13.7
7. Buenos Aires	8.4	7.	Bombay	12.1
8. Paris	8.4	8.	Calcutta	12.1
9. Sao Paulo	7.8	9.	Peking	12.0
10. Osaka	7.6	10.	Osaka	11.8
11. Moscow	7.1	11.	Buenos Aires	11.7
12. Peking	7.0	12.	Rio de Janeiro	11.4

Populations indicated are for greater metropolitan areas.
Figures represent millions of inhabitants.

Assignment 10:C

In the passage below, the noun phrases have been marked like this: -(noun phrase)-
Copy each noun phrase and circle its nucleus. Underline each of the words, phrases, or clauses that modify the nucleus. Then draw arrows from each of the modifiers to the nucleus.

BAD DEAL AT THE TRADING POST*

[1]-(More than 50% of America's farm products)- today consists of -(plants used by the Indians before Columbus planted his flag.)- [2]They include -(beans,)- -(chocolate,)- -(corn,)- -(cotton,)- -(peanuts), -(potatoes,)- -(pumpkins,)- -(tobacco,)- and -(tomatoes.)- [3]-(Botanists)- have yet to discover, in 400 years, -(any medicinal herb that was not used by the Indian.)- [4]That's what they gave us.

[5]Here's -(what we have given them:)- -(high infant mortality rate,)- -(short life expectancy,)- -(dependency on handouts,)- -(loss of pride,)- -(much illness,)- and -(unemployment as high as 80% in some tribes.)- [6]-(The remaining American Indians)- are struggling to hang on to -(the lowest health, education, and economic rungs in American life.)- [7]Somebody had better do something before -(those rungs)- collapse. [8]Remember you're up there somewhere on -(that ladder)- yourself.

*"Bad Deal at the Trading Post," *Newsweek*, February 17, 1969, p. 91. Used by permission.

11. ADVERBS OF FREQUENCY AND PROBABILITY

11.1 Adverbs may be added to any basic sentence pattern.

Adverbs modify verbs, adjectives, and other adverbs.

11.2 **Adverbs of frequency** modify the verb of the sentence. These adverbs show different degrees of frequency. (Adverbs of frequency answer the question "How often?")

Some adverbs of frequency are:

always	occasionally
usually	seldom
often	rarely
frequently	never
sometimes	

Adverbs of frequency are placed in front of time-included verb forms but immediately after time-included aux-words.

Examples:
> Reuben *usually* goes at eight o'clock.
> He *never* misses class.
> He is *seldom* late.
> He has *always* been prompt.

142 SENTENCE CONSTRUCTION

11.3 Adverbs of probability may also be used in this position.

Some adverbs of probability are:

apparently	obviously
certainly	possibly
clearly	probably
evidently	surely

Examples:

He will certainly come. (great probability)
He will probably come. (some probability)

They may also be used before the aux-word and, if emphasis is desired, as front shifters.

Examples:

He certainly will come.
Certainly, he will come.

Assignment 11:A

Write a paragraph about your daily schedule. *Include* at least five adverbs of frequency. *Underline them.*

Assignment 11:B

Write a paragraph about your weekend schedule. *Include* at least five adverbs of frequency. *Underline them.*

Assignment 11:C

Write a paragraph about what your teacher does in class. *Include* at least five adverbs of frequency. *Underline them.*

12. ADVERBS OF INTENSITY

12.1 Adverbs of intensity modify adjectives or other adverbs. They are used to make the meaning of these adjectives or adverbs stronger or more forceful.

Two very common adverbs of intensity are *very* and *extremely*.

They are placed immediately before the adjective or adverb they modify.

Examples:

I am extremely tired.
The package is very big.

12.2 *Too* is an intensifier with a special use. It suggests an undesirable excess of the adjective. It is frequently followed by a phrase beginning with the word *to* (sometimes *for*).

So is another intensifier that in writing is usually followed by a clause beginning with the word *that*.

Examples:

I'm too tired to work anymore.
I'm so tired that I can't work anymore.
The package is too big to fit in the mailbox.
The package is so big that it won't fit in the mailbox.

Note: As can be seen in the examples above, the clauses or phrases which follow *so . . . that* or *too . . to* only have the same meaning when the *so . . that* clause contains a negative. (Without the negative they may even be opposite in meaning.)

Assignment 12:A

Write two additional sentences, one using too *and one using* so *for each sentence below. Follow the pattern given in the model. Write sentences that fit the subjects.*

Model:

Last night Father was very tired.
Last night Father was too tired to eat supper.
Last night Father was so tired that he couldn't eat.

1. Mother was very busy.

2. The children were very noisy.

3. Mother and Father became very upset.

4. Father shouted very loudly.

5. Mother scolded the children very quietly.

6. Suddenly the house was very quiet.

Assignment 12:B

Write two additional sentences, one using too *and one using* so, *for each sentence below. Follow the pattern given in the model. Write sentences that fit the subjects.*

Model:

Last week I saw a very good movie.
The movie was too good to miss.
The movie was so good that I want to see it again.

1. The film was very short.

2. The plot was very scary.

3. The photography was very unusual.

4. The actors were very talented.

5. The theater was very full.

6. The audience clapped very loudly.

7. The show was over very soon.

Assignment 12:C

Write two additional sentences, one using too *and one using* so, *for each sentence below. Follow the pattern given in the model. Write sentences that fit the subjects.*

Model:
    A football game is very exciting.
    A football game is too exciting for some people to watch.
    A football game is so exciting that I scream and yell.

1. The players are very strong.

2. The quarterback passes the ball very swiftly.

3. The linesmen tackle the opposing players very hard.

4. Sometimes the football is very slippery.

5. The football field is very large.

6. The spectators are very happy when their team wins.

13. ADVERBS OF MANNER, PLACE, TIME, ETC.

13.1 **Adverbs of manner** are used to modify verbs or adjectives made from *-ing* or *d-t-n* forms of verbs (see section 6 of this chapter).

These adverbs are normally placed after the verb, or after the object if there is an object. (The alternate position for emphasizing the adverb is before the verb. For example, "*The bird flew away quickly,*" becomes "*The bird quickly flew away,*" when the speed is emphasized.)

Most adverbs of manner are formed by adding *-ly* to an adjective. (A few adverbs of manner such as *fast* and *hard* do not end in *-ly,* and *well* is the adverb form of *good.*)

Some adverbs of manner are:

quickly	suddenly
slowly	thoroughly
carefully	stealthily
wildly	smoothly
precisely	boldly

Examples:

To write English *well* you must write *carefully.*
She gave the speech *quickly.*
The cat crept *stealthily* toward the bird.
The *smoothly* running water flowed over the dam.

13.2 Adverbs of manner (and a few adverbs of frequency) also have **comparative** and **superlative** forms.

The rules for making these forms are the same as those for making comparative and superlative adjective forms. (There are discussed in sections 7 and 8 of this chapter.) Adjectives ending in *-ly* always use *more* and *most* for forming comparatives and superlatives.

Examples:

George runs fast, but Mary runs *faster.*
Mr. Jones reacts quickly, but Mr. Jackson reacts *more quickly.*
I frequently go to town, but George goes *more frequently.*

13.3 **Adverbs of place and time** are usually prepositional phrases. (Some exceptions are *here, there, home, everywhere, anywhere,* and *somehwere* for place, and *yesterday, now,* and *then* for time.)

Some adverbs of time are:

in the morning	after lunch
at night	before breakfast
in the winter	during the semester
since 1933	next week

Examples:

I went shopping at ten o'clock.
I saw Mary in the supermarket.

13.4 When more than one kind (manner, place, or time) of adverb is used, the normal order is manner followed by place followed by time.

Examples:

I saw Mary in the supermarket at ten o'clock. (time)
George studies frantically in the library during the last week of the semester.
    (manner)   (place)   (time)

146 SENTENCE CONSTRUCTION

13.5 Other prepositional phrases which show means, instrument, and purpose are used as adverbs.

Examples:

means	He travels *by train.*
instrument	He made his purchase *with a credit card.*
purpose	He crams *for the test.*

Assignment 13:A

Rewrite the following sentences, inserting adverbs (of the type indicated) in each sentence.

SPORTS ON TV

1. People have some kind of recreation. (adverb of frequency)

2. A few people participate in active sports. (adverb of frequency)

3. The majority prefer to sit and watch others play. (adverb of place)

4. Thousands travel to watch football games. (adverbs of frequency and place)

5. Thousands more watch the same games on TV. (adverbs of manner and place)

6. Admittance to the stadium requires a ticket. (adverb of frequency)

7. Sponsors pay for TV broadcasting. (adverb of frequency)

8. Companies advertise their products during time-outs. (adverb of manner)

9. The only cost for watching is the price of the TV set. (adverb of place)

10. Of course, TV watchers have to endure the commercials. (adverb of manner or place)

Assignment 13:B

Rewrite the following sentences inserting adverbs of the types indicated to each sentence.

THE OLYMPIC GAMES

1. The Olympic Games take place. (adverbs of frequency and place)

2. Summer and winter games attract people. (adverb of place)

3. Amateur athletes from all over the world perform. (adverb of manner)

4. These athletes from all over the world perform. (adverb of manner)

5. These athletes train hard. (adverb of intensity)

6. Spectators watch the various events. (adverb of manner)

7. Athletes break records. (adverbs of frequency and place)

8. The decathlon champion is the world's finest all-around athlete. (adverb of probability)

9. Money for the athletes' expenses comes from private donations. (adverb of frequency or chance)

10. Specific cities or countries provide the accommodations. (adverb of manner)

148 SENTENCE CONSTRUCTION

Assignment 13:C

Rewrite the following sentences inserting adverbs of the types indicated to each sentence.

MY SECRET TALENT

1. I like to sleep. (adverbs of time and frequency)

2. I can sleep. (adverbs of intensity and manner)

3. I sleep with my eyes closed. (adverb of frequency)

4. I am also able to sleep with open eyes. (adverbs of frequency and time or place)

5. Few people can do this. (adverb of manner)

6. It is my greatest talent. (adverb of chance)

7. This talent is useful to me. (adverb of intensity)

8. I couldn't live without it. (adverb of chance)

9. When things are interesting, I listen and watch. (adverb of manner)

10. When boredom sets in, I go to sleep. (adverbs of frequency and manner)

11. Because I don't close my eyes, those around me don't suspect that I am asleep. (adverb of frequency)

12. My only problem is that I snore. (adverb of frequency)

13. If I start to snore, those around me discover my secret. (adverbs of frequency, manner, or chance)

APPENDIX A
CONTENT WORDS

Parentheses indicate words rarely, if ever, used.

NOUN	VERB	ADJECTIVE	ADVERB
ability	enable	able	ably
absence	absent	absent	absently
achievement	achieve	achievable	--------
acquisition	acquire	acquisitive	acquisitively
act, activity, action	act	active	actively
adequacy	--------	adequate	adequately
admission	admit	admissible	admissibly
advantage	--------	advantageous	advantageously
adventure	adventure	adventurous	adventurously
advice	advise	advisory	(advisorily)
aggression	aggress	aggressive	aggressively
aggressor			
allowance	allow	allowable	(allowably)
ambition	--------	ambitious	ambitiously
appreciation	appreciate	appreciative	appreciatively
appropriation	appropriate	appropriate	appropriately
approximation	approximate	approximate	approximately
attention	attend (to)	attentive	attentively
attraction	attract	attractive	attractively
authority	authorize	authoritative	authoritatively
basis	base	basic	basically
benefit	benefit	beneficial	beneficially
bravery	brave	brave	bravely
breadth	broaden	broad	broadly
brilliance	--------	brilliant	brilliantly
capability	--------	capable	capably
capture, captor	capture	captive	(captively)
center	centralize	central	centrally
circle	circle	circular	circularly
clarity	clarify	clear	clearly
cleverness	--------	clever	cleverly

149

NOUN	VERB	ADJECTIVE	ADVERB
comfort	comfort	comfortable	comfortably
competition	compete	competitive	competitively
complex	--------	complex	complexly
comprehension	comprehend	comprehensive	comprehensively
computer	compute	computable	--------
compulsion	compel	compulsive	compulsively
confidence	confide (in)	confident	confidently
consideration	consider	considerable	considerably
construction	construct	constructive	constructively
consumption	consume	consumable	--------
conversion	convert	convertible	(convertibly)
correction	correct	correct	correctly
correctness	correct	correct	correctly
corrector			
corruption	corrupt	corrupt	(corruptly)
courage	encourage	courageous	courageously
criminal, criminality	--------	criminal	criminally
culture	--------	cultural	culturally
curiosity	--------	curious	curiously
danger	endanger	dangerous	dangerously
defense	defend	defensive	defensively
definition	define	definitive	(definitively)
delinquency	--------	delinquent	(delinquently)
dependence, dependent	depend (on)	dependent	dependently
description	describe	descriptive	descriptively
desire	desire	desirable	desirably
destruction	destroy	destructive	destructively
determination	determine	determinable	--------
difference	differ (from)	different	differently
disadvantage	--------	disadvantageous	(disadvantageously)
disaster	--------	disastrous	disastrously
disgrace	disgrace	disgraceful	disgracefully
displeasure	displease	--------	--------
division	divide	divisible	(divisibly)
domination	dominate	dominant	dominantly
doubt	doubt	doubtful	doubtfully, doubtlessly
eagerness	--------	eager	eagerly
education	educate	educational	educationally
effect	effect	effective	effectively
emotion	emote	emotional	emotionally
endurance	endure	endurable	(endurably)
energy	energize	energetic	energetically
enforcement	enforce	enforceable	enforceably
enthusiasm	enthuse	enthusiastic	enthusiastically
equality	equalize	equal	equally
erection	erect	erect	(erectly)
essence, essential	--------	essential	essentially
example	exemplify	exemplary	(exemplarily)
excellence	excel	excellent	excellently
exhaustion	exhaust	exhaustive	exhaustively
expansive	expand	expansive	expansively
exploitation	exploit	exploitable	(exploitably)
extension	extend	extensive	extensively
fame	--------	famous	famously
familiarity	familiarize	familiar	familiarly
fatality	--------	fatal	fatally
favor	favor	favorite	--------
fertility, fertilizer	fertilize	fertile	fertilely

NOUN	VERB	ADJECTIVE	ADVERB
firmness	firm	firm	firmly
force	force	forceful	forcefully
foreigner	--------	foreign	(foreignly)
frankness	--------	frank	frankly
friend, friendliness	befriend	friendly	friendly
gallantry	--------	gallant	gallantly
government	govern	governmental	(governmentally)
gradualness	--------	gradual	gradually
grievance	grieve	grievous	grievously
harshness	harshen	harsh	harshly
haste	hasten	hasty	hastily
hero, heroism	--------	heroic	heroically
ignorance	ignore	ignorant	ignorantly
imagination	imagine	imaginative	imaginatively
immediacy	--------	immediate	immediately
immensity	--------	immense	immensely
impression	impress	impressive	impressively
impossibility	--------	impossible	impossibly
independence	--------	independent	independently
indication	indicate	indicative	(indicatively)
individual, individualism, individuality	individualize	individual(istic)	individually
inevitability	--------	inevitable	inevitably
influence	influence	influential	influentially
insecurity	--------	insecure	insecurely
inspiration	inspire	inspirational	inspirationally
intelligence	--------	intelligent	intelligently
legality	legalize	legal	legally
legislation, legislator, legislature	legislate	legislative	(legislatively)
liberty	liberalize	liberal	liberally
liberty, liberation	liberate	--------	--------
liberality, liberalization	liberalize	liberal	liberally
limitation	limit	limitable	limitably
location	locate	local	locally
looseness	loosen	loose	loosely
loyalty	--------	loyal	loyally
magnet	magnetize	magnetic	(magnetically)
might	--------	mighty	mightily
minimum	minimize	minimal	minimally
movement	move	movable	--------
negation	negate	negative	negatively
notice	notice	noticeable	noticeably
obligation	obligate	obligatory	(obligatorily)
observation, observer	observe	observant	observantly
occasion	occasion	occasional	occasionally
occupation	occupy	occupational	(occupationally)
offense, offender	offend	offensive	offensively
opportunity, opportunist	--------	opportune	opportunely
opposition, opposite	oppose	opposite	(oppositely)
oppression, oppressor	oppress	oppressive	oppressively
optimism, optimist	--------	optimistic	optimistically
part	part	partial	partially
permission, permit	permit	permissive	permissively
perpetuation	perpetuate	perpetual	perpetually
person, personality	personalize	personal	personally
persuasion	persuade	persuasive	persuasively

NOUN	VERB	ADJECTIVE	ADVERB
politics (always pl.), politician	--------	political	politically
possession, possessor	possess	possessive	possessively
poverty	impoverish	poor	poorly
prediction	predict	predictable	predictably
preparation	prepare	preparatory	--------
prevention	prevent	preventive	(preventively)
profit	profit	profitable	profitably
prohibition	prohibit	prohibitive	prohibitively
provision	provide	provisional	provisionally
recurrence	recur	recurrent	recurrently
regularity	regularize	regular	regularly
regulation	regulate	regulative	(regulatively)
relation, relative	relate	relative	relatively
reliance, reliability	rely (on)	reliable	reliably
remedy	remedy	remedial	(remedially)
reminiscence	reminisce	reminiscent	(reminiscently)
respect	respect	respectful, respective	respectfully, respectively
response	respond	responsive	responsively
responsibility	--------	responsible	responsibly
resistance	resist	resistant	(resistantly)
rivalry, rival	rival	rival	--------
satisfaction	satisfy	satisfactory	satisfactorily
scorn	scorn	scornful	scornfully
secrecy	--------	secretive	secretively
section	sectionalize, section	sectional	(sectionally)
sentiment, sentimentality	--------	sentimental	sentimentally
separation	separate	separate	separately
significance	signify	significant	significantly
skill	--------	skillful	skillfully
solemnity	solemnize	solemn	solemnly
steadiness	steady	steady	steadily
strangeness	--------	strange	strangely
student	study	studious	studiously
subsidiary, subsidy	subsidize	subsidiary	--------
success	succeed	successful	successfully
suddenness	--------	sudden	suddenly
suitability	suit	suitable	suitably
suspicion, suspect	suspect	suspicious	suspiciously
swiftness	--------	swift	swiftly
symbol	symbolize	symbolic	symbolically
sympathy	sympathize	sympathetic	sympathetically
system	systematize	systematic	systematically
technique	--------	technical	technically
temporariness	temporize	temporary	temporarily
tightness	tighten	tight	tightly
toleration	tolerate	tolerable	tolerably
transference, transfer	transfer	transferable	--------
treachery	--------	treacherous	treacherously
triumph	triumph (over)	triumphant	triumphantly
tyranny, tyrant	tyrannize	tyrannical	(tyrannically)
uncertainty	--------	uncertain	uncertainly
victory, victor	--------	victorious	victoriously
vigor	invigorate	vigorous	vigorously
virtue	--------	virtuous	virtuously
vitality	vitalize	vital	vitally
violence	--------	violent	violently

APPENDIX B
SOME COMMON NONCOUNT NOUNS AND UNIT EXPRESSIONS

advice (piece, bit)
anger (fit, pique)
beef (piece, slice, side, pound, kilo, serving, platter, helping, can, tin)
beer* (bottle, glass, mug, can, vat, keg)
biology**
catsup (bottle, dab, teaspoon, cup)
chalk (piece, box)
chemistry**
cloth* (yard, bolt, meter, piece, scrap, sample)
cocoa (cup, mug, glass, teaspoon, can, serving)
concrete (yard, bag, wheelbarrow)
corn* (ear, field, bushel, can, kernel)
economics**
entertainment (night, hour)
fabric* (yard, meter, bolt, piece, scrap, sample)
film* (roll, box, package, can, reel)
flour (sack, bag, pound, cup)
fog* (day)
food* (plate, serving, mouthful)
furniture (piece, room, set)
glass* (piece, pane, sheet)
gold (ounce, bar, bag)
grass (field, clump, blade)
gravy (bowl, boat, ladle, pan, serving)
hair* (strand, head, handful)
homework (page)
honey (jar, can, comb, pound)
intelligence (grain, ounce, lick [colloquial])
iron* (ton, pound, truckload, piece)
jealousy (fit, pique, attack)
juice (glass, pitcher, cup, quart, gallon)
junk (piece, pile, truckload)
lamb* (leg, slice, piece, pound, kilo, shoulder)
leather (piece, strip, square inch)
lemonade* (glass, pitcher, cup, quart, gallon)
lettuce (head, leaf)
luggage (piece, set)

lumber (piece, board foot, truckload)
mail (piece, bag, shipment)
material (see *fabric*)
mathematics**
meat (pound, kilo, serving, slice, platter, bite, helping)
medicine* (dose, teaspoon, drop) [also**]
pepper (spoon, pinch, dash)
photography**
pork (serving, slice, roast, loin, side, helping, pound, kilo, platter)
powder (box, can, keg)
pride (ounce)
rain* (inch, drop)
ribbon* (inch, foot, yard, piece)
rice (grain, cup, pound, bag, sack)
salt (spoon, pinch)
sand (grain, bucket, yard)
sight*/***
silver (ounce, bar, bag)
sleet
smell*/***
snow* (inch, foot, ton)
soup (bowl, tureen, ladle, spoonful, can, tin, pot)
stationery (box, ream)
stew* (bowl, tureen, ladle, spoonful, can, tin, pot)
stuff (box, room, load)
sugar (sack, bag, pound, cup, spoon)
tin* (sheet, piece, square inch)
toast* (piece, slice)
toothpaste (tube, tin)
touch*/***
vision*/***
wheat (ton, ear, pound, bag, grain)
wind* (gust)
wine* (bottle, carafe, glass, drop)
wood (cord, piece, load)
work (unit, hour, day, piece, lick)

*These nouns are normally noncount, but they can also be count nouns. When they are count nouns, the meaning is different from the noncount meaning (see p. 10).

**These are areas of study. Unit expressions are not normally used with them. However, unit expressions (area, branch, course, unit, page) relating to courses, books, etc., are sometimes used with them.

***Senses do not normally use unit expressions.

APPENDIX C
IRREGULAR VERB FORMS

	TIMELESS		TIME-INCLUDED		
			Present		Past
Base	d-t-n	-ing	-s form	No-s Form	
be	been	being	is	am, are	was, were
bear	borne, born	bearing	bears	bear	born
beat	beaten, beat	beating	beats	beat	beat
become	become	becoming	becomes	become	became
begin	begun	beginning	begins	begin	began
bend	bent	bending	bends	bend	bent
bet	bet	betting	bets	bet	bet
bite	bitten, bit	biting	bites	bite	bit
bleed	bled	bleeding	bleeds	bleed	bled
blow	blown	blowing	blows	blow	blew
break	broken	breaking	breaks	break	broke
bring	brought	bringing	brings	bring	brought
build	built	building	builds	build	built
burst	burst	bursting	bursts	burst	burst
buy	bought	buying	buys	buy	bought
catch	caught	catching	catches	catch	caught
choose	chosen	choosing	chooses	choose	chose
come	come	coming	comes	come	came
cost	cost	costing	costs	cost	cost
creep	crept	creeping	creeps	creep	crept
cut	cut	cutting	cuts	cut	cut
deal	dealt	dealing	deals	deal	dealt
dig	dug	digging	digs	dig	dug
dive	dived	diving	dives	dive	dived, dove
do	done	doing	does	do	did
draw	drawn	drawing	draws	draw	drew
drink	drunk	drinking	drinks	drink	drank
drive	driven	driving	drives	drive	drove
eat	eaten	eating	eats	eat	ate
fall	fallen	falling	falls	fall	fell
feel	felt	feeling	feels	feel	felt
fight	fought	fighting	fights	fight	fought
find	found	finding	finds	find	found
flee	fled	fleeing	flees	flee	fled
fly	flown	flying	flies	fly	flew
forget	forgotten	forgetting	forgets	forget	forgot
forgive	forgiven	forgiving	forgives	forgive	forgave
freeze	frozen	freezing	freezes	freeze	froze
get	got, gotten	getting	gets	get	got
give	given	giving	gives	give	gave
go	gone	going	goes	go	went

Appendix C

	TIMELESS			TIME-INCLUDED	
				Present	Past
Base	d-t-n	-ing	-s form	No-s form	
grow	grown	growing	grows	grow	grew
hang	hung	hanging	hangs	hang	hung
hang (a person)	hung	hanging	hangs	hang	hanged
have	had	having	has	have	had
hear	heard	hearing	hears	hear	heard
hide	hidden	hiding	hides	hide	hid
hit	hit	hitting	hits	hit	hit
hold	held	holding	holds	hold	held
hurt	hurt	hurting	hurts	hurt	hurt
keep	kept	keeping	keeps	keep	kept
kneel	knelt, kneeled	kneeling	kneels	kneel	knelt, kneeled
know	known	knowing	knows	know	knew
lay	laid	laying	lays	lay	laid
lead	led	leading	leads	lead	led
leave	left	leaving	leaves	leave	left
lend	lent	lending	lends	lend	lent
let	let	letting	lets	let	let
lie (recline)	lain	lying	lies	lie	lay
lie (tell an untruth)	lied	lying	lies	lie	lied
light	lighted, lit	lighting	lights	light	lighted, lit
lose	lost	losing	loses	lose	lost
make	made	making	makes	make	made
mean	meant	meaning	means	mean	meant
meet	met	meeting	meets	meet	met
pay	paid	paying	pays	pay	paid
put	put	putting	puts	put	put
quit	quit	quitting	quits	quit	quit
read	read	reading	reads	read	read
ride	ridden	riding	rides	ride	rode
ring	rung	ringing	rings	ring	rang
rise	risen	rising	rises	rise	rose
run	run	running	runs	run	ran
say	said	saying	says	say	said
see	seen	seeing	sees	see	saw
seek	sought	seeking	seeks	seek	sought
sell	sold	selling	sells	sell	sold
send	sent	sending	sends	send	sent
set	set	setting	sets	set	set
shake	shaken	shaking	shakes	shake	shook
shine (shoes)	shined	shining	shines	shine	shined
shine (sun)	shone	shining	shines	shine	shone
shoot	shot	shooting	shoots	shoot	shot
shrink	shrunk	shrinking	shrinks	shrink	shrank
shut	shut	shutting	shuts	shut	shut
sing	sung	singing	sing	sing	sang
sink	sunk	sinking	sinks	sink	sank
sit	sat	sitting	sits	sit	sat
slay	slain	slaying	slays	slay	slew
sleep	slept	sleeping	sleeps	sleep	slept
wake	waked, woken	waking	wakes	wake	waked, woke
wear	worn	wearing	wears	wear	wore
weave	woven	weaving	weaves	weave	wove
weep	wept	weeping	weeps	weep	weapt
win	won	winning	wins	win	won
wind	wound	winding	winds	wind	wound
wring	wrung	wringing	wrings	wring	wrung
write	written	writing	writes	write	wrote

APPENDIX D
SOME COMMON TWO-WORD VERBS

INSEPARABLE

call on = ask to recite
come back = return
come over = visit
get up = arise
get along = progress
get along with = be friendly, cooperate
get out of = escape, evade
get through = finish
get by = succeed with little effort
get over = recover
go on = happen
go over = review
keep on = continue
look into = investigate
look for = seek
look like = resemble
look out = beware
make out = succeed
make sure of = verify
run over = hit with a car
run out of = exhaust
run across = discover (by chance)
run into = meet (by chance)
show up = appear

SEPARABLE

back up = move to the rear
call up = telephone
do over = repeat
fill out = complete
give back = return
give up = cease, surrender
hand in = submit
hand out = distribute
keep up = maintain
leave out = omit
let go = release
look up = search for
look over = examine
make up = prepare, invent, compensate
make (one's mind) up = decide
pick out = choose
pick up = lift, raise
put away = return to proper place
put off = postpone
put (clothing) on = dress
put out = extinguish
put up = raise
show off = display
take off = remove, undress
take up = introduce, discuss
take down = record in writing